Physical Geography

LOCKYER'S ASTRONOMY.

ELEMENTS OF ASTRONOMY:

Accompanied with numerous Illustrations, a Colored Repre-
sentation of the Solar, Stellar, and Nebular Spectra,
and Celestial Charts of the Northern
and the Southern Hemisphere.

By J. NORMAN LOCKYER.

American edition, revised and specially adapted to the Schools
of the United States.

12mo. 312 pages. Price, $1.50.

The volume is as practical as possible. To aid the student
in identifying the stars and constellations, the fine Celestial
Charts of Arago, which answer all the purposes of a costly Atlas
of the Heavens, are appended to the work—this being the only
text-book, as far as the Publishers are aware, that possesses this
great advantage. Directions are given for finding the most interesting objects in the heavens at certain hours on different
evenings throughout the year. Every device is used to make
the study interesting; and the Publishers feel assured that
teachers who once try this book will be unwilling to exchange
it for any other.

D. APPLETON & CO., PUBLISHERS,

NEW YORK.

SCIENCE PRIMERS, *edited by*

PROFESSORS HUXLEY, ROSCOE, *and* BALFOUR STEWART.

IV.

PHYSICAL GEOGRAPHY.

𝔖𝔠𝔦𝔢𝔫𝔠𝔢. 𝔓𝔯𝔦𝔪𝔢𝔯𝔰.

PHYSICAL
GEOGRAPHY.

BY

Sir ARCHIBALD GEIKIE, LL.D., F.R.S,

Director of the Geological Survey of Scotland, and Murchison-Professor
of Geology and Mineralogy in the University of Edinburgh.

WITH ILLUSTRATIONS.

NEW YORK:
D. APPLETON AND COMPANY,
1, 3, AND 5 BOND STREET.
1880.

CONTENTS.

CONTENTS.

SCIENCE PRIMERS.

PHYSICAL GEOGRAPHY.

INTRODUCTION.

1. LET us suppose that it is summer-time, that you are in the country, and that you have fixed upon a certain day for a holiday ramble. Some of you are going to gather wildflowers, some to collect pebbles, and some without any very definite aim beyond the love of the holiday and of any sport or adventure which it may bring with it. Soon after sunrise on the eventful day you are awake, and great is your delight to find the sky clear and the sun shining warmly. It is arranged, however, that you do not start until after breakfast-time, and meanwhile you busy yourselves in getting ready all the baskets and sticks and other gear of which you are to make use during the day. But the brightness of the morning begins to get dimmed. The few clouds which were to be seen at first have grown large, and seem evidently gathering together for a storm. And sure enough, ere breakfast is well over, the first ominous big drops are seen falling. You cling to the hope that it is only a shower which will soon be over,

and you go on with the preparations for the journey
notwithstanding.   But the rain shows no symptom of
soon ceasing.   The big drops come down thicker and
faster; little pools of water begin to form in the
hollows of the road, and the window-panes are now
streaming with rain.   With sad hearts you have to
give up all hope of holding your excursion to-day

2. It is no doubt very tantalizing to be disappointed,
in this way when the promised pleasure was on the
very point of becoming yours.   But let us see if we
cannot derive some compensation even from the bad
weather.   Late in the afternoon the sky clears a little,
and the rain ceases.   You are glad to get outside
again, and so we all sally forth for a walk.   Streams of
muddy water are still coursing along the sloping roadway.   If you will let me be your guide, I would advise
that we should take our walk by the neighbouring
river.   We wend our way by wet paths and green
lanes, where every hedgerow is still dripping with
moisture, until we gain the bridge, and see the river
right beneath us.   What a change this one day's heavy
rain has made!   Yesterday you could almost count
the stones in the channel, so small and clear was the
current.   But look at it now!   The water fills the
channel from bank to bank, and rolls along swiftly.
We can watch it for a little from the bridge.   As it
rushes past, innumerable leaves and twigs are seen
floating on its surface.   Now and then a larger branch,
or even a whole tree-trunk, comes down, tossing and
rolling about on the flood.   Sheaves of straw or hay,
planks of wood, pieces of wooden fence, sometimes
a poor duck, unable to struggle against the current,
roll past us and show how the river has risen above

its banks and done damage to the farms higher up its course.

3. We linger for a while on the bridge, watching this unceasing tumultuous rush of water and the constant variety of objects which it carries down the channel. You think it was perhaps almost worth while to lose your holiday for the sake of seeing so grand a sight as this angry and swollen river, roaring and rushing with its full burden of dark water. Now, while the scene is still fresh before you, ask yourselves a few simple questions about it, and you will find perhaps additional reasons for not regretting the failure of the promised excursion.

4. In the first place, where does all this added mass of water in the river come from? You say it was the rain that brought it. Well, but how should it find its way into this broad channel? Why does not the rain run off the ground without making any river at all?

5. But, in the second place, where does the rain come from? In the early morning the sky was bright, then clouds appeared, and then came the rain, and you answer that it was the clouds which supplied the rain. But the clouds must have derived the water from some source. How is it that clouds gather rain, and let it descend upon the earth?

6. In the third place, what is it which causes the river to rush on in one direction more than another? When the water was low, and you could, perhaps, almost step across the channel on the stones and gravel, the current, small though it might be, was still quite perceptible. You saw that the water was moving along the channel always from the same quarter. And now when the channel is filled with this rolling torrent of

dark water, you see that the direction of the current is still the same.   Can you tell why this should be?

7. Again, yesterday the water was clear, to-day it is dark and discoloured.   Take a little of this dirty-looking water home with you, and let it stand all night in a glass.   To-morrow morning you will find that it is clear, and that a fine layer of mud has sunk to the bottom.   It is mud, therefore, which discolours the swollen river.   But where did this mud come from? Plainly, it must have something to do with the heavy rain and the flooded state of the stream.

8. Well, this river, whether in shallow or in flood, is always moving onward in one direction, and the mud which it bears along is carried towards the same point to which the river itself is hastening.   While we sit on the bridge watching the foaming water as it eddies and whirls past us, the question comes home to us —what becomes of all this vast quantity of water and mud?

9. Remember, now, that our river is only one of many hundreds which flow across this country, and that there are thousands more in other countries where the same thing may be seen which we have been watching to-day.   They are all flooded when heavy rains come ; they all flow downwards; and all of them carry more or less mud along with them.

10. As we walk homewards again, it will be well to put together some of the chief features of this day's experience.   We have seen that sometimes the sky is clear and blue, with the sun shining brightly and warmly in it ; that sometimes clouds come across the sky, and that when they gather thickly rain is apt to fall.   We have seen that a river flows ; that it is

swollen by heavy rain, and that when swollen it is apt to be muddy. In this way we have learnt that there is a close connection between the sky above us and the earth under our feet. In the morning, it seemed but a little thing that clouds should be seen gathering overhead; and yet, ere evening fell, these clouds led by degrees to the flooding of the river, the sweeping down of trees, and fences, and farm produce; and it might even be to the destruction of bridges, the inundation of fields and villages and towns, and a large destruction of human life and property.

11. But perhaps you live in a large town and have no opportunity of seeing such country sights as I have been describing, and in that case you may naturally enough imagine that these things cannot have much interest for you. You may learn a great deal, however, about rain and streams even in the streets of a town. Catch a little of the rain in a plate, and you will find it to be so much clear water. But look at it as it courses along the gutters. You see how muddy it is. It has swept away the loose dust worn by wheels and feet from the stones of the street, and carried it into the gutters. Each gutter thus becomes like the flooded river. You can watch, too, how chips of straw, corks, bits of wood, and other loose objects lying in the street are borne away, very much as the trunks of trees are carried by the river. Even in a town, therefore, you can follow how changes in the sky lead to changes on the earth.

12. If you think for a little, you will recall many other illustrations of the way in which the common things of everyday life are connected together. As far back as you can remember, you have been familiar with

such things as sunshine, clouds, wind, rain, rivers, frost, and snow, and they have grown so commonplace that you never think of considering about them. You cannot imagine them, perhaps, as in any way different from what they are ; they seem, indeed, so natural and so necessary that you may even be surprised when anyone asks you to give a reason for them. But if you had lived all your lives in a country where no rain ever fell, and if you were to be brought to such a country as this, and were to see such a storm of rain as you have been watching to-day, would it not be very strange to you, and would you not naturally enough begin to ask the meaning of it ? Or suppose that a boy from some very warm part of the world were to visit this country in winter, and to see for the first time snow fall, and the rivers solidly frozen-over, would you be surprised if he showed great astonishment ? If he asked you to tell him what snow is, and why the ground is so hard, and the air so cold, why the streams no longer flow, but have become crusted with ice—could you answer his questions ?

13. And yet these questions relate to very common, everyday things. If you think about them, you will learn, perhaps, that the answers are not quite so easily found as you had imagined. Do not suppose that because a thing is common, it can have no interest for you. There is really nothing so common as not to deserve your attention, and which will not reward you for your pains.

14. In the following pages I propose to ask you to look with me at some of these common things. You must not think, however, that it is my wish merely to set you certain lessons which you have to learn, and

to give you some rudiments of knowledge which you must commit to memory. I would fain have you not to be content with what is said in this little book, or in other books, whether small or great, but rather to get into the habit of using your own eyes and seeing for yourselves what takes place in this wonderful world of ours. All round you there is abundant material for this most delightful inquiry. No excursion you ever made in pursuit of mere enjoyment and adventure by river, heath, or hill, could give you more hearty pleasure than a ramble with eyes and ears alike open to note the lessons to be learnt from every day and from every landscape. Remember that besides the printed books which you use at home, or at school, there is the great book of Nature, wherein each of us, young and old, may read, and go on reading all through life without exhausting even a small part of what it has to teach us.

15. It is this great book—Air, Earth, and Sea— which I would have you look into. Do not be content with merely noticing that such and such events take place. For instance, to return to our walk to the flooded river; do not let a fact such as a storm or a flood pass without trying to find out something about it. Get into the habit of asking Nature questions, as we did in the course of our homeward walk. Never rest until you get at the reasons for what you notice going on around you. In this way even the commonest things will come to wear a new interest for you. Wherever you go there will be something for you to notice; something that will serve to increase the pleasure which the landscape would otherwise afford. You will thus learn to use your eyes quickly

and correctly ; and this habit of observation will be of the utmost value to you, no matter what may be the path of life which lies before you.

16. In the following Lessons I wish to show you what sort of questions you may put about some of the chief parts of the book of Nature, and especially about two of these—the Air and the Earth. Each of us should know something about the air we breathe and the earth we live upon, and about the relations between them. Our walk showed us a little regarding these relations when it enabled us to connect the destruction of fences and farms with the formation of clouds in the sky. Many other relations remain for you to find out. In tracing these you are really busy with science, with that branch of science called Physical Geography, which seeks to describe this earth with all the movements which are going on upon its surface. And yet you are not engaged in anything very difficult or uninteresting. You are simply watching with attentive eyes the changes which are continually taking place around you, and seeking to find out the meaning of these changes, and how they stand related to each other.

THE SHAPE OF THE EARTH.

17. Before observing what takes place on the surface of the earth, it may be well if you form a clear notion about the shape of the whole earth as a mass, and if you fix in your minds some of the great leading features of the connection between the earth and the sun.

18. When you stand in the middle of a broad flat country, or look out upon the wide sea, it seems to

you as if this world on which we live and move were
a great plain, to the edge of which you would come if
you went far enough onward. This is the first notion
we all have as children. It was also the firm belief
of mankind in early times. The sun and moon were
then thought to rise and set only for the use of people
here ; and the sky, with all its stars, was looked upon
as a great crystal dome covering and resting upon
the earth.

19. But you can easily prove to yourselves that the
eye is deceived about the flatness of the earth, and
that what seems quite level is in reality curved. In a
wide level country, such as many parts of the midland
and eastern counties of England, you cannot see trees
and houses farther away than some four or five miles. If
you climb to the top of a church tower, you find many
objects come into sight which you could not have
seen from the ground. And if there should happen
to be a range of hills in the neighbourhood, you would
note from their tops a still larger number of points
which before were hidden. The higher you climb
above the ground, therefore, the further you can see.

20. Again : suppose you were at the bottom of a tall
sea-cliff, and on looking out to sea were to note the
sails of a distant ship. If you mounted to the top of
the cliff, you might see not only the sails, but the
whole vessel, and your eye would probably pick out
ships still further away, appearing as mere specks
along the line of meeting between sea and sky, and
which you could not see at all from the beach.

21. Suppose further, that you were to sit down on the
top of that cliff, and watch these vessels for a time.
Some of them, which at first were so far away that

they could hardly be seen, would probably seem to grow bigger and clearer. You would begin to make out the tops of the masts and sails; by and by the rest of the sails would appear, until at last the hulls too came into sight. These vessels would seem to you to have sailed up over what used to be thought the edge of the world.

FIG. 1.—Disappearance of a Ship at Sea owing to the curved surface of the Earth.

22. On the other hand, some of the ships which were near you at first will gradually sail away towards the same distant parts. Their hulls will dip down into the sea, as it were; then the sails will slowly sink, and in the end all trace of the vessels will have vanished.

23. Now, in making these observations, you will have gathered facts which prove that the world we live in is not a flat plain, but has a curved surface, or in other words is a globe. To use your eyes in this way, and seek out the meaning of that which you see, would neither be a hard nor a dull task; and yet you would really be engaged in what is called observational science. When you watch how the ships at sea appear

to you as they come and go, you observe **facts**. When
you put the facts together, and reason out their connection and meaning, and find that they prove the
roundness of the earth, you make an **induction** or
inference from them. Now it is this union of observation and induction' which makes **science**.

24. You may observe, then, and prove that the old
and natural-enough notion about the flatness of the
earth is quite untrue; and that, flat as the sea and
land may appear, they are only parts of a great curve.
If you·were to set sail from England, and keep sailing
on in the same general direction without turning back,
you would in the end come to England again. You
would sail round the world, and prove it to be actually
a globe. Now, this has often been done. Many voy-
ages have been made round the world, and, instead
of coming to its edge, the voyagers, or "circumnavi-
gators," as they are called, have always found the
land and sea to wear the same curved surface which
we can see for ourselves at home.

25. Though you may find it easy enough to believe
that the surface of the earth is part of a curve when
you look out upon the broad sea, yet when you see
a landscape where the ground is very uneven, such,
for example, as a region of high mountains and deep
valleys, you may find perhaps some difficulty in under-
standing how it can possibly be that such an irregular
surface can be spoken of as part of a curve. In
reality, ·however, the earth is so big, that even the
highest mountains are in comparison merely like little
grains on the surface. It is only when the surface is
level, as on a great plain or on the sea, that we can
usually judge by the eye as to the real form of the

earth.　But even in the most rugged ground the curve is there, though we may fail to notice it.

26. But the curve, after all, is a very gentle one. You can see the vessels at sea for many miles before they sink down out of sight.　The fact that the curve is so gentle shows that the circle of which it forms

Fig. 2.—The Earth and Moon as they would appear seen from the Sun.

part must be of great size.　Now, it has been measured by astronomers, and found to be so big that if a railway train could go completely round the earth at a rate of thirty miles an hour without stoppage, it would take more than a month to complete the circuit.

DAY AND NIGHT.

27. Day by day, as far back as you can remember, you have been accustomed to see the sun travel across the sky. Night after night, when the air has been free from cloud, you have seen the moon and stars sailing slowly overhead. You cannot be more confident of anything than you are that the sun will appear again to-morrow, and move on from year to year as it has done in the past. You have seen that a slow, regular, and unceasing motion seems to be going on all round the earth. Have you ever wondered what can be the cause of this motion?

28. When the sun shines it is warm, when clouds obscure the sky the air is more chilly, and at night, when the sun does not shine at all, we feel a sensation of cold. Again : by day the sky is filled with light, but when the sun sinks in the west darkness begins. You see from this that we depend upon the sun for light and heat. It is evident that we cannot properly understand what takes place upon the earth until we learn something about the relations of the earth to the sun.

29. Perhaps your first impression has been like that of mankind in general long ago. They believed the earth to remain as the fixed central point of the universe, round which sun, moon, and stars were ceaselessly revolving. To this day we speak of these heavenly bodies as **rising** and **setting**, as if we still regarded them as performing a journey round the earth.

30. But instead of being the centre of the universe our earth is in reality only one of a number of heavenly

bodies which travel unceasingly round the sun. The sun is the great central hot mass which warms and lights the earth, and round which the earth is continually circling.

31. The succession of day and night seems to be owing to the movements of the sun, but in reality it is caused by the turning or **rotation** of the earth itself. You can readily illustrate this. Set a humming-top spinning as rapidly as you can. It seems to stand for a while motionless upon its point, but actually it is rotating with great rapidity. Imagine a line passing straight up from the point below, to the top of the stalk above. Every part of the top is spinning round this central line, which is called the **axis of rotation.** In the same kind of way the earth is spinning rapidly on its axis.

32. Again : take an ordinary school-globe, and place a lighted candle a few feet from it, in a line with the brass circle. You can make the globe turn round on its axis. Whether it is allowed to remain at rest or is sent spinning round rapidly, the half of it next the candle is lighted, and the other half away from the candle is in shade. When it is at rest, the places marked on one side remain in the light, while those on the opposite side remain in the dark. As you turn it round, each place in succession is brought round to the light, and carried on into the shade again. And while the candle remains unmoved, the rotation of the globe brings alternate light and darkness to each part of its surface.

33. Instead of the little school-globe in this illustration, imagine our earth, and in place of the feeble candle, the great sun, and you will see how the rotation

of the earth on its axis must bring alternate light and darkness to every country.

34. You must not suppose that there is any actual rod passing through the earth to form the axis round which it turns.   The axis is only an imaginary line, and the two opposite points where it reaches the surface, and where the ends of the rod would come out were the axis an actual visible thing, are called the **North Pole** and the **South Pole.**   They are represented by the two little points by which the school-globe is fixed in its place.

35. Round this axis the earth spins once in every twenty-four hours.   All this time the sun is shining steadily and fixedly in the sky.   But only those parts of the earth can catch his light which happen at any moment to be looking towards him.   There must always be a bright side and a dark side, just as there was a bright side and a dark side when you placed the globe opposite to the candle.   Now you can easily see that if there were no motion in the earth, half of its surface would never see the light at all, while the other half would never be in darkness. · But since it rotates, every part is alternately illuminated and shaded.   When we are catching the sun's light, we have **Day**; when we are on the dark side, we have **Night.**

36. The sun seems to move from east to west.   The real movement of the earth is necessarily just the reverse of this, viz. from west to east.   In the morning we are carried round into the sunlight, which appears in the east.   Gradually the sun seems to climb the sky until we are brought directly opposite to him at noon, and gradually he sinks again to set in

the west, as the earth in its constant rotation bears us round once more into the dark.   Even at night, however, we can still trace the movement of the earth by the way in which the stars one by one rise and set, until their lesser lights are quenched in the returning light of another day.

37. All the time that the earth is rotating on its axis it is circling or **revolving** round the sun.   This motion is called the **revolution** of the earth in its **orbit**. To go completely round the sun, the earth has to travel over so wide a circle or orbit, that it takes rather more than three hundred and sixty-five days to perform the journey, even though it is rushing along at an average speed of about nineteen miles in a second.

38. By the motion of rotation, time is divided into days and nights, by that of revolution it is marked off into years.   So that in this way the earth is our great time-keeper.

THE AIR.

I. What the Air is made of.

39. When we begin to look attentively at the world around us, one of the first things to set us thinking is the air.   We do not see it, and yet it is present wherever we may go.   At one time it blows upon us in a gentle breeze, at another it sweeps along in a fierce storm.   What is this air?

40. Although invisible, it is yet a real, material substance.   When you swing your arm rapidly up and down you feel the air offering a resistance to the hand.   The air is something which you can feel, though you cannot see it.   You breathe it every moment.   You cannot get

away from it, for it completely surrounds the earth. To this outer envelope of air, the name of Atmosphere is given.

41. From the experiments explained in the Chemistry Primer (Art. 9) you learn that the air is not a simple substance, but a mixture of two invisible gases, called nitrogen and oxygen. But besides these chief ingredients, it contains also small quantities of other substances; some of which are visible, others invisible. If you close the shutters of a room, and let the sunlight stream through only one chink or hole into the room, you see some of the visible particles of the air. Hundreds of little motes or specks of dust cross the beam of light which makes them visible against the surrounding darkness, though they disappear in full daylight. But it is the invisible parts of the air which are of chief importance; and among them there are two which you must especially remember—the **vapour of water** and **carbonic acid gas.** You will soon come to see why it is needful for you to distinguish these.

42. Now what is this vapour of water? You will understand its nature if you watch what takes place when a kettle boils. From the mouth of the spout a stream of white cloud comes out into the air. It is in continual motion; its outer parts somehow or other disappear, but as fast as they do so they are supplied by fresh materials from the kettle. The water in the kettle is all the while growing less, until at last, if you do not replenish it, the whole will be boiled away, and the kettle left quite dry. What has become of all the water? You have changed it into vapour. It is not destroyed or lost in any way, it has only passed

from one state into another, from the liquid into the gaseous form, and is now dissolved in the air.

43. Now the air always contains more or less vapour of water, though you do not see it, so long as it remains in the state of vapour. It gives rise to clouds, mist, rain, and snow. If it were taken out of the air, everything would be dried up on the land, and life would be impossible. As you learn more and more of the changes which take place from day to day around you, you will come to see that this vapour of water plays a main part in them all.

44. Carbonic acid gas is also one of the invisible substances of the atmosphere, of which, though it forms no more than four parts in every ten thousand, yet it constitutes an important ingredient. You will understand how important it is when you are told that, from this carbonic acid in the air, all the plants which you see growing upon the land extract nearly the whole of their solid substance (see Chemistry Primer, Art. 11). When a plant dies and decays, the carbonic acid is restored to the air again. On the other hand, plants are largely eaten by animals, and help to form the framework of their bodies. Animals in breathing give out carbonic acid gas; and when they die, and their bodies decay, the same substance is again restored to the atmosphere. Hence the carbonic acid of the air is used to build up the structure both of plants and animals, and is given back again when these living things cease to live. There is a continual coming and going of this material between the air and the animal and vegetable kingdoms (see Chemistry Primer, Art. 13).

II. The Warming and Cooling of the Air.

45. You know that though you cannot see the air you can feel it when it moves. A light breeze, or a strong gale, càn be just as little seen by the eye as still air; and yet we readily feel their motion. But even when the air is still it can make itself sensible in another way, viz. by its **temperature** (see Physics Primer, Art. 51). For air, like common visible things, can be warmed and cooled.

46. This warming and cooling of the air is well illustrated by what takes place in a dwelling-house. If you pass out of a warm room, on a winter's day, into the open air when there is no wind, you feel a sensation of cold. Whence does this sensation come? Not from anything you can see, for your feet, though resting on the frozen ground, are protected by leather, and do not yet feel the cold. It is the air which is cold, and which encircles you on all sides, and robs you of your heat; while at the same time you are giving off or **radiating** heat from your skin into the air (see Physics Primer, Art. 67). On the other hand, if, after standing a while in the chilly winter air you return into the room again, you feel a sensation of pleasant warmth. Here, again, the feeling does not come from any visible object, but from the invisible air which touches every part of your skin, and is thus robbed of its heat by you.

47. Air, then, may sometimes be warm and sometimes cold, and yet still remain quite invisible. By means of the thermometer (which is explained in the Physics Primer, Art. 51), we can measure slight changes of heat and cold, which even the most sensitive skin would fail to detect.

3

48. Now, how is it that the atmosphere should sometimes be warm and sometimes cold? Where does the heat come from? and how does the air take it up?

49. Let us return again to the illustration of the house. In winter, when the air is keen and .frosty outside, it is warm and pleasant indoors, because fires are there kept burning. The burning of coal and wood produces heat, and the heat thus given out warms the air. Hence it is by the giving off or **radiation** of the heat from some burning substance that the air of our houses is made warmer than the air outside.

50. Now, it is really by radiation from a heated body that the air outside gets its heat. In summer, this air is sometimes far hotter than is usual in dwelling-houses in winter. All this heat comes from the sun, which is an enormous hot mass, continually sending out heat in all directions.

51. But, if the sun is always pouring down heat upon the earth, why is the air ever cold? Place a screen between you and a bright fire, and you will immediately feel that some of the heat from the fireplace has been cut off. When the sun is shining, expose your hand to its beams for a time, and then hold a book between the hand and the sun. At first, your skin was warmed; but the moment you put it in the shade, it is cooled again. The book has cut off the heat which was passing directly from the sun to your hand. When the atmosphere is felt to be cold, something has come in the way to keep the sun's heat from directly reaching us.

52. Clouds cut off the direct heat of the sun.

You must often have noticed the change of temperature, when, after the sun has been shining for a time, a cloud comes between it and the earth. Immediately a feeling of chilliness is experienced, which passes off as soon as the cloud has sailed on, and allowed the sun once more to come out.

53. The air itself absorbs some of the sun's heat, and the greater the thickness of air through which that heat has to make its way, the more heat will be

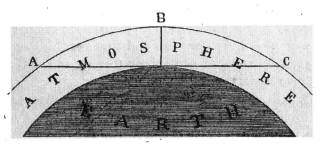

Fig. 3.—Diagram showing the influence of the varying thickness of the atmosphere in retarding the Sun's heat. A. Line of Sun's rays in the morning. B. Line of the rays at noon. C. Line of the rays at sunset.

absorbed. Besides this, the more the rays of heat are slanted the weaker do they become. At noon, for example, the sun stands high in the sky. Its rays (as at B in Fig. 3) are then nearest to the vertical, and have also the least thickness of air to pass through before they reach us. As it descends in the afternoon, its rays get more and more slanted, and must also make their way through a constantly increasing thickness of air (as at C in the diagram). Hence the middle of the day is much warmer than morning or evening.

54. At night, when the sun no longer shines, its heat does not directly warm the part of the earth in shadow. That part not only receives no heat from it, but even radiates its heat out into the cold sky (see Art. 59). Hence night is much colder than day.

55. Then, again, in summer the sun at noon shines much higher in the sky with us, or more directly overhead, than in winter. Its heat comes down less obliquely and has less depth of air to pass through, and hence is much more felt than in winter, when, as you know, the sun in our part of the world never rises high even at midday.

56. From all this it is evident that we get our supplies of heat from the sun, and that anything coming between us and the sun serves to interrupt this heat and give us the sensation of cold.

57. Still, if we were dependent for our warmth upon the direct heat of the sun alone, we should be warm only when the sun shines. A cloudy day would be an extremely cold one, and every night as intensely frosty as it ever is in winter. Yet such is not the case. Cloudy days are often quite warm ; while we are all aware that the nights are by no means always very cold. There must be some way in which the sun's heat is stored up, so that it can be felt even when he is not shining.

58. Let us again have recourse to our first illustration. If you place the back of a chair opposite to the fire, you will find that it gets so hot that you can hardly touch it. Remove the chair to a distant part of the room, and it quickly cools. Hence a part of the heat from the fire has been absorbed by the wood, and again given out.

59. In like manner in summer the ground gets warmed; in some parts, indeed, becoming even so hot at times that we can hardly keep the hand upon it. In hot countries this is felt much more than in Britain. Soil and stones absorb heat readily, that is to say, soon get heated, and they soon cool again. When they have been warmed by the sun, the air gets warmed by contact with them, and keeps its heat longer than they do; so that even when at night the soil and stones have become ice-cold, the air a little above is not so chilly. On the other hand, when the surface of the ground is cold, it cools the air next it. The ground parts easily with its heat, and a vast amount of heat is in this way radiated at night from the earth outward into the cold starry space. Much more heat, however, would be lost from this cause did not the abundant aqueous vapour of the atmosphere (Art. 43) absorb part of it, and act as a kind of screen to retard the radiation. This is the reason why in hot climates, where the air is very dry—that is, contains a small proportion of the vapour of water—the nights are relatively colder than they are in other countries where the air is moister. In like manner, clouds serve to keep heat from escaping; and hence it is that cloudy nights are not so cold as those which are clear and starry.

60. The atmosphere, then, is heated or cooled according as it lies upon a warm or cold part of the earth's surface; and, by means of its aqueous vapour, it serves to store up and distribute this heat, keeping the earth from such extremes of climate as would otherwise prevail.

III. What happens when Air is warmed or cooled—Wind.

61. The air lying next to a hot surface is heated; the air touching a cold surface is cooled. And upon such differences of temperature in the air the formation of winds depends.

62. Hot or warm air is lighter than cold air. You have learnt how heat expands bodies (Physics Primer, Art. 49). It is this expansion of air, or the separation of its particles further from each other, which makes it less·dense or heavy than cold air, where the particles lie more closely together. As a consequence of this difference of density, the light warm air rises, and the heavy cold air sinks. You can easily satisfy yourselves of this by experiment. Take a· poker, and heat the end of it in the fire until it is red-hot. Withdraw it, and gently bring some small bits of very light paper or some other light substance a few inches above the heated surface. The bits of paper will be at once carried up into the air. This happens because the air heated by the poker immediately rises, and its place is taken by colder air, which, on getting warmed, like-wise ascends. The upward currents of air grow feebler as the iron cools, until, when it is of the same temperature as the air around, they cease.

63. This is the principle on which our fireplaces are constructed. The fire is not kindled on the hearth, for, in that case, it would not get a large enough draught of air underneath, and would be apt to go out. It is placed some way above the floor, and a chimney is put over it. As soon as the fire is lighted, the air next it gets warmed, and begins to mount, and the air in the room is drawn in from below to take the

place of that which rises. All the air which lies above the burning coal gets warmer and lighter; it therefore flows up the chimney, carrying with it the smoke and gases.` You will understand that though a bright blazing fire is a pleasant sight in winter, we do not get all the heat which it gives out. On the contrary, a great deal of the heat goes up the chimney; and, except in so far as it warms the walls, passes away and warms the outer air.

64. What happens in a small way in our houses takes place on a far grander scale in nature. As already pointed out (Art. 50), the sun is the great source of heat which warms and lightens our globe. While the heat of the sun is passing through the air, it does very little in the way of warming it. The heat goes through the air, and warms the surface of the earth. You know that in summer the direct rays of the sun are hot enough to burn your face, and yet, if you put even a thin sheet of paper over your head, enough to cut off these rays, the sensation of burning heat at once goes off, although the same air is playing about you all the time.

65. Both land and water are heated by the sun's rays, and the same change in the air then takes place which we find also at our firesides. The layer of air next the warmed earth becomes itself warmed. As it thereby grows lighter it ascends, and its place is taken by colder air, which flows in from the neighbourhood to take its place. This flowing in of air is **Wind**.

66. It is easy for you now and then to watch how wind arises. Suppose, for instance, that during the summer you spend some time at the sea-coast. In the morning and early part of the day a gentle wind will

often be noticed, blowing from the land out to sea. As the day advances, and the heat increases, this wind dies away. But after a while, when the day is beginning to sink towards evening, another breeze may be noticed springing up from the opposite quarter, and blowing with a delicious coolness from the sea to the land. These breezes are the result of the unequal heating and cooling of the sea and land.

67. Let us understand how this takes place. On a hot day you find that stones, soil, or other parts of the land get very warm under the sun's rays ; yet if you bathe in the sea at that time you feel its waters to be pleasantly cool. This shows that the land becomes more quickly hot than the sea. After such a hot day you will find that at night the surface of the land becomes much colder than the sea, because it parts with its heat sooner than the sea does. By day the hot land heats the air above it, and makes it lighter, so that it ascends ; while the cooler and heavier air lying on the sea flows landward as a cool and re-freshing sea-breeze. By night this state of things is just reversed; for then the air which lies on the chilled land being colder and heavier than that which covers the warmer sea, flows seaward as a cool land-breeze.

68. Take a school-globe, and notice some of the lines which are drawn round it. Midway between the two poles you will notice a line running round the most projecting part of the globe. This line is called the **equator**. It divides the globe, as you see, into two halves or hemispheres. Now, over the parts of the earth which this line traverses, and for some way on either side, the sun shines with intense heat all the

year round. The air is constantly heated to a high degree, and streams upwards in ascending currents. But just as the hot air along this central belt mounts up into the higher regions of the atmosphere, the cooler air from north and south flows in along the surface to supply its place. This constant streaming of air into the equatorial regions forms what are known as the Trade Winds. The steadiness of these winds, and the way in which they may be counted upon in navigation, led long ago to their being called by their present name.

69. In our country the winds are by no means so regular and constant. If you look at the map, and mark the position of Britain upon the surface of the earth, you will readily notice some obvious reasons why our winds should be variable. To the west lies the wide Atlantic Ocean; to the east, beyond the narrow and shallow North Sea, stretches the vast continental mass of Europe and Asia. Seas and lands much colder than ours lie to the north ; others much warmer than ours spread to the south. So that, with so variable a surface receiving the sun's heat, we may be quite prepared to find that sometimes a warm wind blows from one quarter, and sometimes a cold wind from another.

IV. The Vapour in the Air. Evaporation and Condensation.

70. One of the most important ingredients in the air was stated in Art. 41, to be the vapour of water. Let us try to see, first of all, how it gets into and out of the air. And in this case, as before, you will find that great questions in science often admit of being

simply and readily illustrated by the most familiar
things.

71. In a warm room, where a good fire has been
burning all day, and a number of people· have been
gathered together, you might suppose that the air must
be tolerably dry.   But bring a tumbler of ice-cold
water into the room, and mark what happens to it.
You will see the outside of the glass immediately
covered with a fine film of mist.   In a little while
minute drops of water will form out of this film, and
will go on growing, until, p(rhaps, some of them unite
and trickle down the side of the tumbler.

72. You may have noticed, too, that on very cold
nights the windows of sitting-rooms or crowded public
halls are apt to be found streaming with water on the
inside.

73. Now, in such cases, where does the moisture
come from ?   Certainly not out of the glass.   It is
derived from the vapour of water present in the air.
This word vapour is often used to describe some kind
of visible mist or fog.   But these visible forms of moisture are not properly vapour in the sense in which the
term is used in science.   The aqueous vapour of the
air is always invisible, even when the air is saturated
with it, and only when it passes back into the state of
water do you actually see anything.

74. When the invisible vapour dissolved in the
air becomes visible, as in mists, clouds, dew, or rain,
it is said to be **condensed,** ·and this process of
liquefaction is called **condensation.**

75. The quantity of vapour which the air can
contain varies according to temperature, warm air
being able to hold more than cold air.   You can show

this in a simple way.   In breathing you exhale at each breath a quantity of aqueous vapour; when the air is warm, this invisible vapour, as soon as it escapes from you, mixes with the outer air, and is kept dissolved there.   But if you cool the breath as it leaves your mouth, the vapour is at once condensed into visible moisture.   Take a mirror, for example, or any other cold surface, and breathe on it; the vapour from your lungs at once shows itself in a film of mist upon the glass, because the air in contact with the cold surface is chilled and cannot hold so much vapour, part of which is condensed.   During winter you do not need a mirror to make the vapour of the breath visible, for the cold air around you at once condenses this vapour as it comes from the mouth, and forms the fine cloud or mist which appears with each breath that you exhale.

76.   As the air is cooled, its power of retaining vapour diminishes.   When it becomes colder than the temperature at which it is able to keep its supply of vapour dissolved, the excess of vapour is condensed and becomes visible.   The temperature at which this takes place is the point of saturation, or Dew-point (see Art. 85).

77. Perhaps you may ask how it is that the vapour so universally present gets into the atmosphere, and where it comes from.   If you pour a little water into a plate, and set it down in the open air, you will note, in the course of a day or two, that the water has sensibly diminished.   The air has drunk up part of it, and will drink up the whole, if the water is allowed to stand long enough.   What takes place from a small quantity of water goes on from every

surface of water on the face of the earth, from every brook and river and lake, and from the great sea itself. Water is constantly passing off into vapour which is received and retained by the air. This process is called **Evaporation,** and the water which passes off into vapour is said to **evaporate.**

78. Since warm air can hold more vapour than cold air, evaporation must be more vigorous in sunshine than at night, and during summer than during winter. You have often noticed a great difference in the rate at which wet roads will dry up. When the sun shines warmly upon them, an hour or two may be enough to drive off all the moisture from them, and make them white and hard again. But if the weather is cold and dull, they may remain wet and damp for days together. In the one case the warm air greedily absorbs the vapour of the water on the roads ; in the other, the cold air takes up the vapour only in small quantities.

79. Again, on a dry bracing day evaporation goes on rapidly, because the air has not nearly got all the quantity of vapour it can hold in solution. On a damp day, however, when the air contains about as much vapour as it can hold at that particular temperature, evaporation is quite feeble, or ceases altogether. This varying capacity of the air for vapour is the reason why laundresses find so much difference between days, in the ease with which they can have their clothes dried. On some days the air is busy drinking up vapour everywhere, and then the clothes dry quickly. Such is especially the case when the sky is clear and the wind blows, because every moment a fresh quantity of air comes in contact with the clothes, carries off some of the vapour, and passes on

to make way for fresh supplies of thirsty air. On other days, the air can hardly hold any more vapour; and the clothes are found at the end of the day to be almost as wet as when they were hung out in the morning.

80. When water evaporates, the vapour carries away some of the heat of the water with it. Put a drop of water on the back of your hand, and let it evaporate; you notice a sensation of cold, because in evaporating the vapour has robbed your skin of some of its heat. This abstracted heat is given out again into the air, when the vapour is condensed.

81. You see, then, that the air contains invisible aqueous vapour, which though very small in quantity, when compared with the amount of nitrogen and oxygen, is yet enormous when the whole mass of the atmosphere is considered; that this vapour rises from every water-surface over the whole earth by the process of evaporation, and that it is brought back again into the liquid form by the process of condensation.

V. Dew, Mist, Clouds.

82. After sunset, when the sky is clear, you know that the grass gets wet with dew. In the morning you may see mists hanging over woods, and streams, and hills, and gradually melting away as the sun mounts in the sky. At all times of the year you may watch how clouds form and dissolve, and form again, ever changing their size and shape as they move through the air. Now these are all examples of the condensation of vapour. Let us see how the process takes place.

83. Condensation, as we have seen (Art. 76), results

4

from a cooling of the air. When vapour is condensed,
it does not at once take the form of running water.
The cold glass brought into the warm room has first
a fine film of mist formed upon it, and then by
degrees the clear drops of water come. In reality
mist is made up of exceedingly minute particles of
water, and it is the running together of these which
makes the larger drops. So in nature on the great scale,
when condensation occurs the vapour first appears
as a fine mist. This is always the result of cooling;
so that, whenever you see a mist or cloud forming,
you may conclude that the air in which it lies is being
cooled.

84. **Dew.**—This name is given to the wetness
which we notice appearing in the evening or at night
upon grass, leaves, or stones, or even sometimes on
our hair. In the morning you have, no doubt, often
watched the little dewdrops sparkling upon the foliage
and the delicate threads of gossamer. Now this wetness does not come out of the leaves or stones, nor
out of your hair. It is all derived from the air by
condensation, exactly as we saw the film of mist form
upon the cold tumbler in the warm moist air of a
room. In fact, that film of mist was really dew, and
all dew is formed in the same way, and from the same
cause.

85. At night, when the sky is clear, the earth radiates heat rapidly; that is to say, it gives off into cold
space a great part of the heat which it has received
from the sun during the day (Art. 59). Its surface
consequently becomes cold, as you may have felt
when you put your hand upon leaves or stones after
nightfall. The layer of air next the cooled ground is

chilled below its point of condensation, and the excess of vapour is deposited as dew upon the grass, twigs, stones, and other objects. Hence it is that the temperature at which this condensation begins to take place is called the **Dew-point** (Art. 76).

86. **Mist and Fog.**—Another way in which a cold surface of the earth may produce condensation is shown by what takes place among mountains. When a warm moist wind blows upon a chill mountain top, the air is cooled, and its vapour becomes visible in the form of a mist or cloud. You can often see that the cloud is quite solitary, and even shapes itself to the form of the ground, as if it were a sort of fleecy cap drawn down over the mountain's head. This is often well marked in the morning. As day advances, the ground, warmed by the sun, no longer cools the air, and hence the mist is gradually re-absorbed into the atmosphere. But by and by, at the coming on of night, when the ground is once more cooled by radiation, if there should be vapour enough in the air, the mist will re-form, and the mountain put on his cap again.

87. Cold air, as well as cold ground, condenses the vapour of warmer air. If you watch what goes on along the course of a river, you will often see examples of this kind of condensation. The ground on either side of the river parts with its heat after sun-down sooner than the river itself does, and consequently cools the air above it more than the air above the river is cooled. So when this colder air from either side moves over to take the place of the warmer damp air lying on and rising from the river, condensation ensues in the form of the mist or river-

fog, which so commonly hangs at night and early morning over streams.

88. **Clouds.**—It is not on the ground, however, but up in the air that the chief condensation of vapour takes place. No feature of everyday occurrence is more familiar to you than the clouds, which are the result of this condensation. A cloud is merely a mist formed by the cooling of warm moist air when it loses its heat from any cause, such as expansion during ascent, or contact with currents of cooler air. If you watch what goes on in the sky, you may often see clouds in the act of forming. At first a little flake of white appears. By degrees this grows larger, and other cloudlets arise and flock together, until at last the sky is quite overcast with heavy clouds, and rain begins to fall. The vapour which is thus condensed in the air has all been obtained by the evaporation of the water on the earth's surface. It rises with the warm air, which losing its heat as it ascends, and coming too in contact with colder layers of the atmosphere, cannot hold all its vapour, and is obliged to get rid of the excess, which then condenses into cloud.

89. On a summer morning the sky is often free from cloud. As the day advances, and the earth gets warmed, more vapour is raised ; and as this vapour, borne upward by the ascending air-currents, reaches the higher and colder parts of the atmosphere, it is chilled into the white fleecy clouds which you see forming about midday and in the afternoon. Towards evening, when less evaporation takes place, the clouds cease to grow, and gradually lessen in size until at night the sky is quite clear. They have been dis-

solved again by descending and coming in contact with the warm air nearest to the earth. Again, you have often noticed that clouds move across the sky. They are driven along by upper currents of air, and of course the stronger these currents are the faster do the clouds travel. In this way the sky is sometimes completely overcast with clouds which have come from a distance. By watching these comings and goings of the clouds, you see how the state of the vapour in the atmosphere continually changes. At one time it is condensed into clouds, at another time evaporated and made invisible by the varying currents of the air.

VI. Where Rain and Snow come from.

90. You have now traced the vapour which the sun's heat raises from the rivers, lakes, and seas of the earth, and you have found it to be condensed again into visible form in the clouds. But the clouds do not remain always suspended in the sky. Sometimes they melt away again, and are dissolved into invisible vapour. But they often disappear in another way. They let their moisture fall through the air to the earth, and thus give rise to rain and snow.

91. **Rain.**—You are well aware that rain always comes from clouds in the sky. When the sky is clear overhead, no rain falls. Only when it gets overcast does the rain come. You can watch a dark rain-cloud gather itself together and discharge a heavy shower upon the earth. In the illustration of the cold glass brought into the warm room (Art. 71), you remember that the film of mist formed upon the glass was found by degrees to gather into drops,

which trickled down the cold surface. Now the mist on the glass and the cloud in the sky are both formed of minute particles of water separated by air. It is the running together of these particles which gives rise to the drops. In the one case, the drops run down the cold glass. In the other case, they fall as drops of rain through the air. Rain therefore is thus a further stage in the condensation of the aqueous vapour of the atmosphere. The minute particles of the cloud, as condensation proceeds, gather more moisture round them, until at last they form drops of water too heavy to hang any longer suspended in the air. These then fall to the earth as rain-drops.

92. **Snow.**—But there is another important form in which the moisture of the clouds may descend to the surface of the earth. When the weather is cold enough, there fall to the ground not drops of rain, but flakes of snow.

93. If you bring snow indoors, it soon melts into water. If you expose this water for a time it evaporates. Snow, water, and aqueous vapour are thus only different forms of the same substance. We say that water can exist in three forms,—the gaseous, the liquid, and the solid. Snow is an example of the solid condition.

94. On a frosty night pools of water are covered with a hard transparent crust of what is called **Ice.** You may break this crust into pieces, but if the cold continues, a new crust will soon be formed with bits of the old one firmly cemented in it. And the greater the cold the thicker will the crust be, until perhaps the whole of the water in the pools may become solid. If you take a piece of this solid substance, you find it to be cold, brittle, and transparent. Brought into

a warm room it soon melts into water, and you may drive off the water as before into vapour. Ice is the general name given to water when it is in the solid state, such forms as snow and hail being only different appearances which ice puts on. Whenever water becomes colder than a certain temperature it passes into ice, or **freezes,** and this temperature is consequently known as the **freezing-point** (Physics Primer, Art. 51).

95. You might suppose that ice is but a shapeless thing. But gather a few snowflakes, and, that they may not melt, examine them out of doors. When they lie

FIG. 4.—Forms of Snowflakes.

together in a mass they have a pure opaque whiteness, but in reality they are as transparent as water; and it is only from the way in which they scatter the light from their many glistening points, that they appear white. To assure yourselves of this fact, carefully separate one or two of the flakes upon some dark surface (the sleeve of a coat will do well), and you will find that each flake is a more or less perfect star with six rays, formed of little needles or crystals of pure transparent ice. The flakes are so delicate that in falling through the air they are apt to be damaged by coming against each other. Some of their varieties are shown in Fig. 4.

96. The upper layers of the atmosphere are much

colder than the freezing-point of water.   In the condensation which takes place there, the clouds do not
resolve themselves into rain. The vapour of the up-
streaming currents of warm air from the earth's surface
is condensed and frozen in these high regions, and
passes into little crystals, which unite into flakes of
snow.   Even in summer the fine white cloudlets which
you see floating at great heights are probably formed
of snow.   But in those countries, such as ours, where
in winter the air even at the surface is sometimes very
cold, the snow falls to the ground, and lies there as a
white covering, until returning warmth melts it away.

97. Besides rain and snow, the moisture of the air
takes sometimes the form of **Hail**, which consists of
little lumps of ice like frozen rain ; and of **Sleet**, which
is partially melted snow.   But rain and snow are the
most important, and it is these two forms which we
must follow a little further.

98. **Summary.**—Before doing so, let us gather together the sum of what has been said about the aqueous
vapour of the air.   We have learnt that, as every
sheet of water on the face of the globe evaporates, the
air is full of vapour ; that this vapour is condensed into
visible form, and appears as dew, mist, and cloud.
We have learnt further, that the vapour of which
clouds are formed is resolved into rain and snow,
and, in one or other of these forms, descends to the
earth again.   There is thus a circulation of water
between the solid earth beneath and the air above.
This circulation is as essential to the earth in making
it a fit habitation for living things, as the circulation of
blood is in keeping our bodies alive.   It mixes and

washes the air, clearing away impurities, such as those which rise from the chimneys of a town. It moistens and quickens the soil, which it renders capable of supporting vegetation. It supplies springs, brooks, and rivers. In short, it is the very mainspring of all the life of the globe. So important a part of the machinery of the world deserves our careful consideration. Let us next attend, therefore, to what becomes of the rain and the snow after they have been discharged from the air upon the surface of the earth.

THE CIRCULATION OF WATER ON THE LAND.

I. What becomes of the Rain.

99. Although air is continually evaporating water from the surface of the earth, and continually restoring it again by condensation, yet, on the whole and in the course of years, there seems to be no sensible gain or loss of water in our seas, lakes, and rivers; so that the two processes of evaporation and condensation balance each other.

100. It is evident, however, that the moisture precipitated at any moment from the air is not at once evaporated again. When a shower of rain falls, the roads are not dry the moment the shower is over. And when heavy rain continues for hours together, the whole country round may be flooded, and will, perhaps, remain so for days after the rain has ceased. The disappearance of the water is due in part to evaporation, but only in part. A great deal of it goes out of sight in other ways.

101. The rain which falls upon the sea is the

largest part of the whole rainfall of the globe, because the surface of the sea is about three times greater than that of the land. All this rain gradually mingles with the salt water, and can then be no longer recognized. It thus helps to make up for the loss which the sea is always suffering by evaporation. For the sea is the great evaporating surface whence most of the vapour of the atmosphere is derived.

102. On the other hand, the total amount of rain which falls upon all the land of the globe must be enormous. It has been estimated, for example, that about 68 cubic miles of water annually descend as rain even upon the surface of the British Isles, and there are many much more rainy regions than ours. If you inquire about this rain which falls upon the land, you will find that it does not at once disappear, but begins another kind of circulation. Watch what happens during a shower of rain. If the shower is heavy, you will notice little runnels of muddy water coursing down the streets or roads, or flowing out of the ridges of the fields. Follow one of the runnels. It leads into some drain or brook, that into some larger stream, the stream into a river ; and the river, if you follow it far enough, will bring you to the sea. Now think of all the brooks and rivers of the world, where this kind of transport of water is going on, and you will at once see how vast must be the part of the rain which flows off the land into the ocean.

103. But does the whole of the rain flow off at once into the sea in this way? Assuredly not, as you can very easily prove. Suppose that before the rain came the ground had been very dry, and that after the shower you dig up a spadeful of earth. Do you find

the ground dry now? No; because some of the rain has soaked into the earth. And if you could dig deep enough, or if you were to notice what goes on when workmen are making a deep excavation, you would find that the ground underneath is not merely damp, but that it contains plenty of water, and that you could collect this water, and bring it up to the surface. Clearly, then, a good deal of the rain which falls upon the land must sink underground and gather there. You may think that surely the water which disappears in that way must be finally withdrawn from the general circulation which we have been tracing. When it sinks below the surface, how can it ever get up to the surface again?

104. Yet, if you consider for a little, you will be convinced that whatever becomes of it underneath it cannot be lost. If all the rain which sinks into the ground were for ever removed from the surface circulation, you will at once see that the quantity of water upon the earth's surface must be constantly and visibly diminishing. The seas must be getting narrower and shallower; the rivers and lakes must be drying up. But no such changes, so far as can be seen, are really taking place. The sea rolls as broadly and deeply as it has done for many generations past, and the lakes and rivers remain very much the same. So that if any of the water which sinks into the earth is never restored to the surface again, it must be so small a part as to make no sensible difference on the amount which is restored. In spite of the rain which disappears into the ground, the circulation of water between the air, the land, and the sea continues without perceptible diminution.

105. You are driven to conclude, therefore, that there must be some means whereby the water underground is brought back to the surface. This is done, as you will learn in the next section, by **Springs,** which gush out of the earth, and bring up water to feed the **Brooks** and **Rivers,** whereby it is borne into the sea.

106. You can now answer the question, What becomes of the Rain? Most of it sinks into the earth, and afterwards comes out again in springs; part of it is collected into brooks and rivers; and this part, in so far as not evaporated, works its way over the land and falls at last into the sea.

107. Here, then, are two distinct courses which the rainfall takes—one below ground, and one above. It will be most convenient to follow the underground portion first.

II. How Springs are formed.

108. In this Lesson we are to follow the course of that part of the rain which sinks below ground. A little attention to the soils and rocks which form the surface of a country is enough to show that they differ greatly from each other in hardness, and in texture or grain. Some are quite loose and porous, others are tough and close-grained. They consequently differ much in the quantity of water they allow to pass through them. A bed of sand, for example, is **pervious**; that is, will let water sink through it freely, because the little grains of sand lie loosely together, touching each other only at some points, so as to leave empty spaces between. The water readily finds its way among these empty spaces. In fact, the sand-

bed may become a kind of sponge, quite saturated with the water which has filtered down from the surface. A bed of clay, on the other hand, is **impervious**; it is made up of very small particles fitting closely to each other, and therefore offering resistance to the passage of water. Wherever such a bed occurs, it hinders the free passage of the water, which, unable to sink through it from above on the way down, or from below on the way up to the surface again, is kept in by the clay, and forced to find another line of escape.

109. Sandy soils are dry because the rain at once sinks through them; clay soils are wet because they retain the water, and prevent it from freely descending into the earth.

110. When water from rain or melted snow sinks below the surface into the soil, or into rock, it does not remain at rest there. If you were to dig a deep hole in the ground, you would soon find that the water which lies between the particles would begin to trickle out of the sides of your excavation, and gather into a pool in the bottom. If you baled the water out, it would still keep oozing from the sides, and the pool would ere long be filled again. This would show you that the underground water will readily flow into any open channel which it can reach.

111. Now the rocks beneath us, besides being in many cases porous in their texture, such as sandstone, are all more or less traversed with cracks—sometimes mere lines, like those of a cracked window-pane, but sometimes wide and open clefts and tunnels. These numerous channels serve as passages for the underground water. Hence, although a rock may be so

hard and close-grained that water does not soak
through it at all, yet if that rock is plentifully supplied
with these cracks, it may allow a large quantity of
water to pass through. Limestone, for example, is a
very hard rock, through the grains of which water can
make but little way; yet it is so full of cracks or
"joints," as they are called, and these joints are often
so wide, that they give passage to a great deal of
water.

112. In hilly districts, where the surface of the
ground has not been brought under the plough, you
will notice that many places are marshy and wet, even
when the weather has long been dry. The soil everywhere around has perhaps been baked quite hard by
the sun ; but these places remain still wet, in spite of
the heat. Whence do they get their water? Plainly
not directly from the air; for in that case the rest
of the ground would also be damp. They get it
not from above, but from below. It is oozing out
of the ground; and it is this constant outcome of
water from below which keeps the ground wet and
marshy. In other places you will observe that the
water does not merely soak through the ground,
but gives rise to a little runnel of clear water. If
you follow such a runnel up to its source, you
will see that it comes gushing out of the ground as
a **Spring.**

113. Springs are the natural outlets for the underground water. But you ask, why should this water
have any outlets, and what makes it rise to the
surface?

114. The following diagram (fig. 5) represents the
way in which many rocks lie with regard to each other,

and in which you would meet with them if you were to cut a long deep trench or section beneath the surface. They are arranged, as you see, in flat layers or beds. Let us suppose that *a* is a flat layer of some impervious rock, like clay, and *b* another layer of a porous material, like sand.   The rain which falls on the surface of the ground, and sinks through the upper bed, will be arrested by the lower one, and made either to gather there, or find its escape along the surface of that

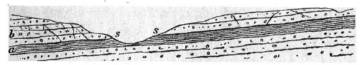

FIG. 5. – Origin of Surface Springs.

lower bed. If a hollow or valley should have its bottom below the level of the line along which the water flows, springs will gush out along the sides of the valley, as shown at *s s* in the woodcut.   The line of escape may be either, as in this case, the junction between two different kinds of rock, or some of the numerous joints already referred to.   Whatever it be, the water cannot help flowing onward and downward, as long as there is any passage by which it can find its way; and the rocks underneath are so full of cracks, that it has no difficulty in doing so.

115. But it must happen that a great deal of the underground water descends far below the level of the valleys, and even below the level of the sea.   And yet, though it should descend for several miles, it comes at last to the surface again.   To realize clearly how this takes place, let us follow a particular drop of water from the time when it sinks into the earth as

rain, to the time when, after a long journeying up and down in the bowels of the earth, it once more reaches the surface. It soaks through the soil together with other drops, and joins some feeble trickle, or some more ample flow of water, which works its way through crevices and tunnels of the rocks. It sinks in this way to perhaps a depth of several thousand feet

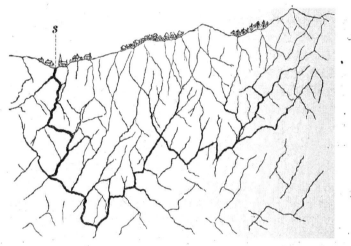

FIG. 6.—Section of part of a district to show the origin of deep-seated Springs. The numerous joints in the rocks lead the water down into a main channel, by which it re-ascends to the surface as a spring at *s*.

until it reaches some rock through which it cannot readily make further way. All this while it has been followed by other drops, coursing after it through its winding passage down to the same barrier at the bottom. The union of all these drops forms an accumulation of water, which is continually pressed by what is descending from the surface. Unable to work its way downward, the pent-up water must try to find escape in some other direction. By the pressure from above it is driven through other cracks and passages, winding up and down until at last it comes to the surface again. It breaks out there as a gushing spring (see Physics Primer, Art. 23).

116. Thus each of the numerous springs which issue out of the ground is a proof that there is a circulation of water underneath, as well as upon the surface of the land. But besides these natural outlets, other proofs are afforded by the artificial openings made in the earth. Holes, called **Wells**, are actually dug to catch this water. Mines, pits, quarries, and deep excavations of any kind, are usually troubled with it, and need to be kept dry by having it pumped out.

III. The work of Water underground.

117. No form of water seems purer than the clear crystal spring as it comes bubbling out of the earth. Water, perfectly pure in a chemical sense, should consist only of the two elements Oxygen and Hydrogen. But in the water of every spring, no matter how clear and sparkling it may be, there is something else. If you take a quantity of perfectly pure water and boil it down, you may drive the whole of it off in steam, and not a vestige of anything is left behind. Rain takes up a little impurity from the air, yet may be regarded as very nearly pure water. But if you boil down a quantity of spring water, you find a residue of solid matter. Sparkling transparency is thus no guide to the chemical purity of the water (see Chemistry Primer, Arts. 20, 21).

118. If now rain is water nearly in a state of purity, and if after journeying up and down underground it

comes out again in springs, always more or less mingled
with other materials, it must get these materials from
the rocks through which it travels. They are not
visible to the eye, for they are held in what is called
chemical solution (Chemistry Primer, Art. 23). When
you put a few grains of salt or sugar upon a plate, and
pour water over them, they are dissolved in the water,
and disappear. They enter into union with the water.
You cannot see them, but you can still recognize their
presence by the taste which they give to the water
which holds them in solution.

119. So water, sinking from the soil downwards, dissolves a little of the substance of the subterranean
rocks, and carries this dissolved material up to the
surface of the ground. But you may say, salt and
sugar are easily acted on by water, hard rocks are
not; how is it that the springs can get their solid impurities from rocks?

120. You remember that one of the important ingredients in the air is carbonic acid gas, and that this substance is both abstracted from and supplied to the air
by plants and animals (see Art. 44). In descending
through the atmosphere rain absorbs a little air. As
ingredients of the air, a little carbonic acid gas, particles
of dust and soot, noxious vapours, minute organisms,
and other substances floating in the air, are caught up
by the descending rain, which in this way, as it were,
washes the air, and tends to keep it much more whole-
some than it would otherwise be.

121. But rain not merely picks up impurities from
the air, it gets a large addition when it reaches the
soil. When you take up a little earth from a field
or a garden, you may notice tiny fibres and decaying

roots in it. It contains always more or less organic matter, and therefore (Art. 44) carbonic and some other acids. If you put some of the soil on a piece of iron and thrust it into the fire, you will burn off the organic matter, remove the carbonic acid, and change the colour of the soil.

122. Armed with the carbonic acid which it gets from the air, and with the larger quantity which it abstracts from the soil, rain-water is prepared to attack rocks, and to eat into them in a way which pure water could not do (see Chemistry Primer, Experiment 28).

123. Water containing carbonic acid has a remarkable effect on many rocks, even on some of the very hardest. It dissolves more or less of their substance, and removes it. When it falls for instance on chalk or limestone, it almost entirely dissolves and carries away the rock in solution, though still remaining clear and limpid. In countries where chalk or limestone is an abundant rock, this action of water is sometimes singularly shown in the way in which the surface of the ground is worn into hollows. In such districts, too, the springs are always **hard**; that is, they contain much mineral matter in solution, whereas rain-water and springs which contain little impurity are termed **soft** (Chemistry Primer, Art. 26).

124. Many of the substances abstracted from below by the water of springs are useful in the life of plants and of animals. Lime, salt, and iron, for example, are all brought up in spring-water, and are all of great value. Lime furnishes material for the bones of animals, and iron supplies the colouring matter of their blood. We obtain, indeed, most of what we need of these materials from our solid food; yet spring-

water, in so far as it contains them, is healthier for drinking and cooking than rain-water would be.

125. As every spring throughout the world is busy bringing up materials of some kind to the surface,

FIG 7.—Subterranean Channel dissolved out of Limestone-rock by Water.

it is plain that the amount of rock dissolved and removed must in the end be very great. You can now see how there should be open channels and

tunnels for the water underground, for the water is
always eating away a little of the surface over which
it flows, thereby widening the cracks and crevices,
and converting them by degrees into wider passages.
In this way large caverns many feet high and many
miles long have been formed underneath the surface
in different parts of the world.

IV. How the surface of the Earth crumbles away.

126. When a stone building has stood for a few
hundred years, the smoothly dressed face which its
walls received from the mason is usually gone. The
stones are worn into holes and furrows, the carvings
over window and doorway are so wasted that perhaps
you cannot make out what they were meant to repre-
sent. This time-eaten character of old masonry is so
familiar that one always looks for it in an old building,
and when it is absent he at once doubts whether the
building can really be old.

127. Again, in the burying-ground surrounding a
venerable church you see the tombstones more and
more mouldered the older they are. Sometimes,
especially in towns, the inscriptions dating from more
than a few generations back are so greatly wasted
that you cannot now tell whose names and virtues
they were set up to commemorate.

128. This crumbling away of hard stone with the
lapse of time is a common familiar fact to you. But
have you ever wondered why it should be so? What
makes the stone decay, and what purpose is served by
the process?

129. In the case of buildings and other works of

human construction the decay can be noted and measured, for the stones, rough and worn as they may be now, left the hands of the masons with smoothly dressed surfaces. But the decay is not confined to human erections. On the contrary, it goes on over the whole face of the world.

130. It may seem so strange to you to be told that the surface of the earth is crumbling away that you should take every opportunity of verifying the statement. Examine all the old buildings and pieces of sculpture within your reach. Look at the cliffs and ravines, the crags and watercourses, in your neighbourhood. At the base of each cliff you will probably find the ground cumbered with blocks and heaps of lesser fragments which have fallen from the rocks above, and after a frosty winter you may even find the fresh scar whence a new mass has been detached to add to the pile of ruins below.

131. After examining your own district in this way, you will, no doubt, find proofs that, in spite of their apparent steadfastness, even the hardest stones are really crumbling down. In short, wherever rocks are exposed to the air they are liable to decay. Now let us see how this change is brought about.

132. First of all we must return for a moment to the action of **carbonic acid,** which has been already (Art. 123) described. You remember that rain-water abstracts a little carbonic acid from the air, and that, when it sinks under the earth, it is enabled by means of the acid to eat away some parts of the rocks beneath. The same action takes place with the rain, which rests upon or flows over the surface of the ground. The rain-water dissolves out little by little

such portions of the rocks as it can remove. In the case of some rocks, such as limestone, the whole, or almost the whole, of the substance of the rock is carried away in solution. In other kinds, the portion dissolved is the cementing material whereby the mass of the rock was bound together; so that when it is taken away, the rock crumbles into mere earth or sand, which is readily washed away by the rain. Hence one of the causes of the mouldering of stone is the action of the carbonic acid taken up by rain.

133. In the second place, the **oxygen** of the portion of air contained in rain-water helps to decompose rocks. When a piece of iron has been exposed for a time to the weather, in such a damp climate as that of Britain, it rusts. You know how, in the course of years, iron railings get quite eaten through, and how you can scrape the dirty yellow crust or powder from the corroded surfaces. This rust is a compound substance, formed by the union of oxygen with iron. It continues to be formed as long as any of the unrusted iron remains, since as each crust of rust is washed off a new layer of iron is laid open to the attacks of the oxygen. What happens to an iron railing or a steel knife, happens also, though not so quickly nor so strongly, to many rocks. They, too, rust by absorbing oxygen. A crust of corroded rock forms on their surface, and, when it is knocked off by the rain, a fresh layer of rock is reached by the ever-present and active oxygen.

134. In the third place, the surface of many parts of the world is made to crumble down by means of **frost**. You are, no doubt, acquainted with some of the effects of frost. You have, probably, noticed that

sometimes during winter, when the cold gets very keen, pipes full of water burst, and jugs filled with water are cracked from top to bottom.   The reason of this lies in the fact that water expands in freezing. Ice requires more space than the water would do if it remained fluid.   When ice forms within a confined space, it exerts a great pressure on the sides of the vessel, or cavity, which contains it.   If these sides are not strong enough to bear the strain to which they are put, they must yield, and therefore they crack (see Physics Primer, Art. 61).

135. You have now learnt how easily rain finds its way through soil.   Even the hardest rocks are more or less porous, and take in some water.   Hence, when winter comes, the ground is full of moisture; not in the soil merely,. but in the rocks.   And so, as frost sets in, this pervading moisture freezes.   Now, precisely the same kind of action takes place with each particle of water, as in the case of the burst water-pipe or the cracked jar.   It does not matter whether the water is collected into some hole or crevice, or is diffused between the grains of the rocks and the soil.   When it freezes it expands, and in so doing tries to push asunder the walls between which it is confined.

136. Hence arise some curious and interesting effects of frost upon the ground.   If you walk along a road just after frost, you see that the small stones have been partly pushed out of their beds, and that the surface of the road is now a layer of fine mud. The frost has separated the grains of sand and clay, as if they had been pounded down in a mortar. Hence frost is of great service to the farmer in break-

ing up the soil, and opening it out for the roots and
fibres of plants. When a surface of rock has been
well soaked with rain, and is then exposed to frost,
the grains of the rock undergo the same kind of pressure from the freezing of the water in the pores
between them. They are not so loose and open, however, as those of the soil are, and they withstand the
action of the frost much better. Of course, the most
porous rocks, or those which hold most water, are
most liable to the effects of this action. Porous
rocks, such as sandstone, are often liable to rapid
decay from frost. The stone has crust after crust
peeled off from it; or its grains are loosened from
each other and washed away by rain.

137. Again, water freezes not only between the com-
ponent grains, but in the numerous crevices or joints,
as they are called, by which rocks are traversed. You
have, perhaps, noticed that on the face of a cliff, or in
a quarry, the rock is cut through by lines running
more or less in an upright direction, and that by
means of these lines the rock is split up by nature,
and can be divided by the quarryman into large four-
sided blocks or pillars. These lines, or joints, have
been already (Art. 111) referred to as passages for
water in descending from the surface. You can understand that only a very little water may be admitted
at a time into a joint. But by degrees the joint widens
a little, and allows more water to enter. Every time
the water freezes it tries hard to push asunder the two
sides of the joint. After many winters, it is at last
able to separate them a little; then more water enters,
and more force is exerted in freezing, until at last the
block of rock traversed by the joint is completely split

up. When this takes place along the face of a cliff, one of the loosened parts may fall off and actually·roll down to the bottom of the precipice.

138. This kind of waste is represented in the accompanying woodcut (Fig. 8), which gives a section of

FIG. 8 —Waste of a Cliff.

a cliff wherein the rocks are traversed by perpendicular joints. These have been, widened along the front until large blocks have been wedged off and have fallen to the ground.   In countries exposed to severe winters, the waste caused by frosts along lines of steep cliff is often enormous.

139. In addition to carbonic acid, oxygen, and frost, there are still other influences at work by which the surface of the earth is made to crumble.   For example, when, during the day, rocks are highly heated by strong sunshine, and then during night are rapidly cooled by radiation, the alternate expansion and contraction caused by the extremes of temperature loosen the particles of the stone, causing them to crumble away, or even making successive crusts of the stone fall off.

140. Again; rocks which are at one time well soaked with rain, and at another time are liable to be dried by the sun's rays and by wind, are apt to crumble away.

141. And thus you see that from a variety of causes the solid rocks of the earth are liable to continual decay and removal.   The hardest stone, as well as the softest, must yield in the end, and moulder down.   They do not all indeed decay at the same rate.   If you look more narrowly at the wall of an ancient building, you will see almost every variety in the degree of decay. Some of the stones are hardly worn at all, while others are almost wholly gone.   As this takes place in a building, you may be sure it must take place also in nature, and that cliffs or crags formed of one kind of stone will crumble down faster than others, and will do so in a different kind of way.

142. If then it be true, as it is, that a general wasting of the surface of the land goes on, you may naturally ask why this should be.   The world seems

so fair and beautiful, that you cannot perhaps realize
to yourselves that there should be so much decay on
its surface.   You may be even inclined at first to consider the decay as a misfortune hardly to be explained.
But instead of being a misfortune, the mouldering of
the surface is in reality necessary to make the earth
fit to be the dwelling-place of plants and animals.
To it we owe the scooping out of valleys, and ravines,
and the picturesque outlines of crags and hills.   Out
of the crumbled stones all soil is made, and on the
formation and renewal of the soil we depend for our
daily food.   How this is brought about will be told
in the next Lesson.

V. What becomes of the crumbled parts of Rocks. How Soil is made.

143. Take up a handful of soil from any field or
garden, and look at it attentively.   What is it made
of? You see little pieces of crumbling stone, particles
of sand and clay, perhaps a few vegetable fibres;
and the whole soil has a dark colour from the
decayed remains of plants and animals diffused
through it.   Now let us in the present Lesson try to
learn how these different materials have been brought
together.

144. We return again to the general mouldering of
the surface of the land.   The words "decay," "waste,"
and others of similar meaning, are applied to this process.   But in reality, although the rocks may crumble
away, and thereby grow less in size year by year, there
is no actual loss of material to the surface of the earth.
The substance of the rock may decay, but it is not
destroyed.   It only changes its condition and its form.

What, then, becomes of all this material which is continually being worn from the rocks around us?

145. Every drop of rain which falls upon the land helps to alter the surface. You have followed the **chemical** action of rain when it dissolves parts of rocks. It is by the constant repetition of the process, drop after drop, and shower after shower, for years together, that the rocks become so wasted and worn. But the rain has also a **mechanical** action.

146. Watch what happens when the first pattering drops of a shower begin to fall upon a smooth surface of sand, such as that of a beach. Each drop makes a little dint or impression. It thus forces aside the grains of sand. On sloping ground, where the drops

FIG. 9.—Prints impressed on Clay or Sand by Drops of Rain.

can run together and flow downward, they are able to push or carry the particles of sand or clay along. This is called a mechanical action; while the actual solution of the particles, as you would dissolve sugar or salt, is a chemical action. Each drop of rain may act in either or both of these ways.

147. Now you will readily see how it is that rain does so much in the destruction of rocks. It not only dissolves out some parts of them, and leaves a crumbling crust on the surface, but it washes away this crust, and thereby exposes a fresh surface to decay.

There is in this way a continual pushing along of
powdered stone over the earth's surface. Part of this
material accumulates in hollows, and on sloping or
level ground ; part is swept into the rivers, and carried
away into the sea.

148. It is this crumbled stone of which all our soils
are made, mingled with the remains of plants and
animals. Soils differ, therefore, according to the kind
of rock out of which they have been formed. Sandstone, for example, will give rise to a sandy soil ;
limestone to a limy or calcareous soil ; clay-rocks to a
clayey soil.

149. But for this crumbling of the rocks into soil,
the land would not be covered with verdure as it is.
Bare sheets of undecaying stone would give no foot-
ing for the roots of plants. But by the decay of their
surface, they get covered with fertile soil, all over the
valleys and plains ; and only where, as in steep banks
and cliffs, they rise too abruptly to let their crumbled
remains gather round them, do they stand up naked
and verdureless.

150. As the mouldering of the surface of the land is
always going on, there is a constant formation of soil.
Indeed, if this were not the case, if after a layer of
soil had been formed upon the ground, it were to
remain there unmoved and unrenewed, the plants
would by degrees take out of it all the earthy materials
they could, and leave it in a barren or exhausted
state. But some of it is being slowly carried away
by rain, fresh particles from mouldering rocks are
washed over it by the same agent, while the rock or
sub-soil underneath is all the while decaying into
soil. The loose stones, too, are continually crumbling

down and making new earth. And thus, day by day, the soil is slowly renewed.

151. Plants, also, help to form and renew the soil. They send their roots among the grains and joints of the stones, and loosen them. Their decaying fibres supply most of the carbonic acid by which these stones are attacked, and furnish also most of the organic matter in the soil. Even the common worms, which you see when you dig up a spadeful of earth, are of great service in mixing the soil and bringing what lies underneath up to the surface.

152. When we think about this decay and renewal of soil, we see that in reality the whole surface of the land may be looked upon as travelling downward or seaward. The particles worn from the sides and crests of the high mountains may take hundreds or thousands of years on the journey; they may lie for a long time on the slopes; they may then be swept down and form part of the soil of the valleys; thence they may be in after years borne away and laid down on the bed or bank of a river; and thus, after many halts by the way, they at last reach the sea.

153. In order to form some idea of the extent to which the surface of the land is cleared of its loose soil by rain, you should notice what takes place even in this country after every series of heavy showers. Each little runnel and brook becomes muddy and discoloured from the quantity of soil, that is, decayed rock, which is washed into it by the rain from the neighbouring slopes. The mud which darkens the water is made of the finer particles of the decomposed rocks; the coarser parts are moving along at the bottom of the water. When you watch these streamlets at

their work, and when you remember that what they are doing now they have been doing for ages past, you will understand how greatly the surface of a country may come to be changed by the action of what at first seems so insignificant a thing as Rain.

VI. Brooks and Rivers. Their Origin.

154. We must now go back to an earlier Lesson (Art. 107), where the way in which rain is disposed of was referred to. You remember that one part of the rain sinks under the ground, and you have traced its progress there until it comes to the surface again. You have now to trace, in a similar way, the other portion of the rainfall which flows along the surface in brooks and rivers.

155. You cannot readily meet with a better illustration of this subject than that which is furnished by a gently sloping road during a heavy shower of rain. Let us suppose that you know such a road, and that just as the rain is beginning you take up your station at some part where the road has a well-marked descent. At first you notice that each of the large heavy drops of rain makes in the dust, or sand, one of the little dints or rain-prints already described (Art. 146). As the shower gets heavier these rain-prints are effaced, and the road soon streams with water. Now mark in what manner the water moves.

156. Looking at the road more narrowly, you remark that it is full of little roughnesses—at one place a long rut, at another a projecting stone, with many more inequalities which your eye could not easily detect when the road was dry, but which the water at once discloses. Every little dimple and projection

affects the flow of the water. You see how the raindrops gather together into slender streamlets of running water which course along the hollows, and how the jutting stones and pieces of earth seem to turn these streamlets now to one side and now to another.

157. Towards the top of the slope only feeble runnels of water are to be seen. But further down they become fewer in number, and at the same time larger in size. They unite as they descend; and the larger and swifter streamlets at the foot of the descent are thus made up of a great many smaller ones from the higher parts of the slope.

158. Now this sloping roadway, with its branching rills of rain, coursing down the slope, and uniting into larger streams as they advance, shows very well the way in which the rain runs off the sloping surface of a country or a continent, and we shall return to the illustration again.

159. Why does the water run down the sloping road? why do rivers flow? and why should they always move constantly in the same direction? They do so for the same reason that a stone falls to the ground when it drops out of your hand; because they are under the sway of that attraction towards the centre of the earth, to which, as you know, the name of **Gravity** (Physics Primer, Art. 4) is given. Every drop of rain falls to the earth because it is drawn downwards by the force of this attraction. When it reaches the ground it is still, as much as ever, under the same influence; and it flows downwards in the readiest channel it can find. Its fall from the clouds to the earth is direct and rapid; its descent from the mountains to the sea, as

part of a stream, is often long and slow ; but the cause of the movement is the same in either case. The winding to and fro of streams, the rush of rapids, the roar of cataracts, the noiseless flow of the deep sullen currents, are all proofs how paramount is the sway of the law of gravity over the waters of the globe,

160. Drawn down in this way by the action of gravity, all that portion of the rain which does not sink into the earth must at once begin to move down-wards along the nearest slopes, and continue flowing until it can get no further. On the surface of the land there are hollows called **Lakes,** which arrest part of the flowing water, just as there are hollows on the road which serve to collect some of the rain. But in most cases they let the water run out at the lower end as fast as it runs in at the upper, and therefore do not serve as permanent resting places for the water. The streams which escape from lakes go on as before, work-ing their way to the sea-shore. So that the course of all streams is a downward one ; and the sea is the great reservoir into which the water of the land is continually pouring.

161. If the surface of a country were a mere long smooth ridge, like the roof of a house, the rain would quickly flow down on either side into the sea. But this is by no means the general character of the surface of the land. Mountains, hills, valleys, gorges, and lakes give a most uneven and varied outline. But besides these greater inequalities which strike the eye at once, even places which seem at first quite level have usually some slope or some slight unevennesses ; just as on the road you found that there may be many little irregu-larities of surface, which you would not notice until

the rain found them out. Water is thus a most accurate measurer of the levels of a country. It will not flow up a slope, but always seeks the lowest level it can find.

162. You can see, then, that though the rain should fall equally over the whole surface of a country, it cannot flow equally over that surface, because the ground is uneven, and the rain runs off into the hollows. It is this unevenness which makes the rain collect into brooks, and these into rivers.

163. The brooks and rivers of a country are thus the natural drains, by which the surplus rainfall, not required by the soil or by springs, is led back again into the sea. When we consider the great amount of rain, and the enormous number of brooks in the higher parts of the country, it seems, at first, hardly possible for all these streams to reach the sea without overflowing the lower grounds. But this does not take place; for when two streams unite into one, they do not require a channel twice as broad as either of their single water-courses. On the contrary, such an union often gives rise to a stream which is not so broad as either of the two from which it flows. But it becomes swifter and deeper. In this way thousands of streamlets, as they come together in their descent, are made to take up less and less room, until the surplus waters of a whole vast region are borne into the sea by one single river-channel.

164. Let us return to the illustration of the roadway in rain. Starting from the foot of the slope, you found the streamlets of rain getting smaller and smaller, and when you came to the top there were none at all. If, however, you were to descend the road on the other

side of the ridge, you would probably meet with other streamlets coursing down-hill in the opposite direction. At the summit the rain seems to divide, part flowing off to one side, and part to the other.

165. In the same way, were you to ascend some river from the sea, you would watch it becoming narrower as you traced it inland, and branching more and more into tributary streams, and these again subdividing into almost endless little brooks. But take any of the branches which unite to form the main stream, and trace it upward. You come, in the end, to the first beginnings of a little brook, and going a little further you reach the summit, down the other side of which all the streams are flowing to the opposite quarter. The line which separates two sets of streams in this way is called the **Water-shed.** In England, for example, one series of rivers flows into the Atlantic, another into the North Sea. If you trace upon a map a line separating all the upper streams of the one side from those of the other, that line will mark the water-shed of the country.

166. But there is one important point where the illustration of the road in rain quite fails. It is only when rain is falling, or immediately after a heavy shower, that the rills are seen upon the road. When the rain ceases the water begins to dry up, till in a short time the road becomes once more firm and dusty. But the brooks and rivers do not cease to flow when the rain ceases to fall. In the heat of summer, when perhaps there has been no rain for many days together, the rivers still roll on, smaller usually than they were in winter, but still with ample flow. What keeps them full? If you remember what you have

already been told about underground-water, you will answer that **rivers are fed by springs as well as by rain.**

167. Though the weather may be rainless, the springs continue to give out their supplies of water, and these keep the rivers going. But if great drought comes, many of the springs, particularly the shallow ones, cease to flow, and the rivers fed by them shrink up or get dry altogether. This is the case with the rivers of this country, which are all, comparatively speaking, very small. The great rivers of the globe, such as the Mississippi, drain such vast territories, that any mere local rain or drought makes no sensible difference in their mass of water.

168. In some parts of the world, however, the rivers are larger in summer and autumn than they are in winter and spring. The Rhine, for instance, begins to rise as the heat of summer increases, and to fall as the cold of winter comes on. This happens because the river has its source among snowy mountains. Snow melts rapidly in summer, and the water which streams from it finds its way into the brooks and rivers, which are thereby greatly swollen. In winter, on the other hand, the snow remains unmelted ; the moisture which falls from the air upon the mountains is chiefly snow; and the cold is such as to freeze the brooks. Hence the supplies of water at the sources of these rivers are, in winter, greatly diminished, and the rivers themselves become proportionately smaller.

169. **Summary.**—To sum up what has been stated in this and the preceding Lessons regarding the circulation of water :—From the highest parts of the land

7

down to the sea, water is continually travelling downward. It does not pour over the whole surface, but
gathers into the hollows, where it forms streams which
wind to and fro, always seeking a lower level, till at
last they lose themselves in the sea. From the sea
vapour is constantly rising into the air, whence it is
brought back and condensed upon the land as rain
or snow, which feeds the streams that flow downward
into the sea. This circulation of water goes on without ceasing.

VII. Brooks and Rivers. Their work.

170. In the first lesson of this little book you were
asked to watch. the doings of a river. Let us now
again return to the same scene, but before the storm
which was then described. The river is not yet swollen
with the sudden and heavy rain. It flows gently over
its pebbly channel, not covering the whole of it, perhaps, but leaving banks of gravel and pools of water
between which the clear current, much diminished by
drought, winds its way. The river seems to be doing
nothing else than lazily carrying the surplus water of
the land towards the sea. You might be surprised to
be told that it has any work to do, and even now is
doing it.

171. But consider whence the water of the river
comes. We have found that it is largely derived from
springs, and that all spring-water contains more or less
mineral materials dissolved out of the brooks. Every
river, therefore, is carrying not merely water, but large
quantities of mineral matter into the sea. It has been
calculated, for instance, that the Rhine in one year
carries into the North Sea lime enough to make three

hundred and thirty-two thousand millions of oyster shells. This chemically-dissolved material is not visible to the eye, and in no way affects the colour of the water. At all times of the year, as long as the water flows, this invisible transport of some of the materials of rocks must be going on.

172. But let us now again watch the same river in flood. The water is no longer clear, but dull and dirty. Yõu ascertained that this discoloration arises from mud and sand suspended in the water. You may stand for hours and watch the swollen, turbid torrent rolling down its channel. During that time many tons of gravel, sand, and mud must be swept past you. You see that over and above the mineral matter in chemical solution, the river is hurrying seaward with vast quantities of other and visible materials. And thus it is clear that at least one great part of the work of rivers must be to transport the mouldered parts of the land which are carried into them by springs or by rain.

173. But the rivers, too, help in the general destruction of the surface of the land. Of this you may readily be assured, by looking at the sides or bed of a stream when the water is low. Where the stream flows over hard rock, you find the rock all smoothed and ground away; and the stones lying in the water-course are all more or less rounded and smoothed. When these stones were originally broken by frosts or otherwise, from crags and cliffs, they were sharp-edged, as you can prove by looking at the heaps of blocks lying at the foot of any precipice, or steep bank of rock. But when they fell, or were washed into the river, they began to get rolled and rubbed, until their sharp edges

were ground away, and they came to wear the smooth rounded forms which we see in the ordinary gravel.

174. While the stones are ground down, they, at the same time, grind down the rocks which form the

FIG. 10.—Potholes excavated by a Stream in the Rocks of its Bed.

sides and bottom of the river-channel over which they are driven. You can even see in some of the eddies of the stream how the stones are kept moving round

until they actually excavate deep round cavities, called
pot-holes, in the solid rock. When the water is low,
as during the droughts of summer, some of these cavities are laid bare, and you may then observe how well
they have been polished. Their general appearance
is shown in Fig. 10.

175. Now, it is clear that two results must follow
from this ceaseless wear and tear of rocks and stones
in the channel of a stream. In the first place, a great
deal of mud and sand must be produced; and, in the
second place, the bed of the river must be ground
down so as to become deeper and wider. The sand
and mud are added to the other similar materials
washed into the streams by rain from the mouldering
surface of the land. By the deepening and widening
of the water-courses, such picturesque features as
gorges and ravines are excavated out of the solid
rock.

176. You have now seen why the rivers are muddy.
Let us inquire what becomes of all the mud, sand,
gravel, and blocks of stone which they are continually
transporting.

177. Look, again, at the channel of a river in summer. You see it covered with sheets of gravel in one
place, beds of sand in another, while here and there
a piece of hard rock sticks up through these different
kinds of river-stuff. Note some portion of the loose
materials, and you find it to be continually shifting. A
patch of gravel or sand may remain for a time, but
the little stones and grains of which it is made up
are always changing as the water covers and moves
them. In fact, the loose materials over which the river
flows are somewhat like the river itself. You come

back to its banks after many years, and you find the river there still, with the same ripples, and eddies, and gentle murmuring sound.   But though the river has been there constantly all the time, its water has been changing every minute, as you can watch it changing still.   So, although the channel is always more or less covered with loose materials, these are not always the same.   They are perpetually being pushed onward, and others, from higher up the stream, come behind to take their place.

178. It is not in the bottoms of the rivers, then, that the material worn away from the surface of the land can find any lasting rest.   And yet the rivers do get rid of a good deal of this material as they roll along.   You have, perhaps, noticed that a river is often bordered with a strip of flat plain, the surface of which is only a few feet above the level of the water.   Most of our rivers have such margins, and, indeed, seem each to wind to and fro through a long, level, meadow-like plain.   Now this plain is really made up from the finer particles of the decomposed rocks which the river has carried along.   During floods, the river, swollen and muddy, rises above its banks, and spreads over the low ground on either side.   Whenever this takes place, the overflowing water moves more slowly over the flats ; and, as its current is thus checked, it cannot hold so much mud and sand, but allows some of these materials to settle down to the bottom.   In this way the overflowed tracts get a coating of soil laid over them by the river, and when the waters retire this coating adds a little to the height of the plain.   The same thing takes place year after year, until by degrees the plain gets so far raised that the river, which all this

while is also busy deepening its channel, cannot over-
flow it even at the highest floods.   In course of time
the river, as it winds from side to side, cuts away
slices of the plain and forms a newer one at a lower
level. And thus a series of terraces is gradually made,
rising step by step above the river.

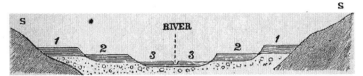

Fig. 11.—Section of the successive terraces (1, 2, 3) of sand, earth, and
gravel formed by a River along a valley (s—s).

179. Still the laying down of its sand and mud by
a river to form one or more such river-terraces is,
after all, only a temporary disposal of these materials.
They are still liable to be carried away, and in truth
they are carried off continually as the river eats away
its banks.

180. When the current of a river is checked as it
enters the sea or a lake, the feebler flow of the water
allows the sand and mud to sink to the bottom.   By
degrees some portions of the bottom come in this
way to be filled up to the surface of the river, and
wide flat marshy spaces are formed on either side of
the main stream.   During floods these spaces are
overflowed with muddy water, in the same way as in
the case of the valley plains just described, and a
coating of mud or sand is laid down on them until
they slowly rise above the ordinary level of the river,
which winds about among them in endless branching
streams.   Vegetation springs up on these flat swampy
lands ; animals, too, find food and shelter there ; and

thus a new territory is made by the work of the
river.

181. These flat river-formed tracts are called Deltas,
because the one which was best known to the ancients,
that of the Nile, had the shape of the Greek letter
Δ (*delta*).   This is the general form which is taken

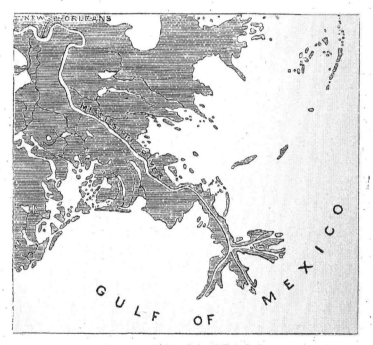

FIG. 12.—Delta of the Mississippi.

by accumulations at the mouths of rivers; the flat
delta gets narrow towards the inland, and broader
towards the sea.   Some of them are of enormous
size; the delta of the Mississippi, for example.

182. Each delta, then, is made of materials worn
from the surface of the land, and brought down by the

river. And yet vast though some of these deltas are, they do not show all the materials which have been so worn away. A great deal is carried far out and deposited on the sea-bottom ; for the sea is the great basin into which the spoils of the land are continually borne.

VIII. Snow-fields and Glaciers.

183. Having now followed the course taken by the water which falls on the land as rain, we come to that taken by snow (Art. 92).

184. On the tops of some of the highest mountains in Britain snow lies for great part of the year. On some of them, indeed, there are shady clefts wherein you may meet with deep snow-wreaths even in the heat of summer. It is only in such cool and sheltered spots, however, that the snow remains unmelted.

185. But in other parts of Europe, where the mountains are more lofty, the peaks and higher shoulders of the hills gleam white all the year with unmelted snow. Hardly anything in the world will impress you so much as the silence and grandeur of these high snowy regions. Seen from the valleys, the mountains look so vast and distant, so white and pure, yet catching up so wonderfully all the colours which glow in the sky at morn or even, that they seem to you at first rather parts of the heaven above than of the solid earth on which we live. But it is when you climb up fairly into their midst that their wonderful stateliness comes full before you. Peaks and pinnacles of the most dazzling whiteness glisten against the dark blue of the sky, streaked here and there with lines of purple shadow, or with knobs of the dark rock projecting

through the white mantle which throws far and wide
its heavy folds over ridge and slope, and sends long
tongues of blue ice down to the meadows and vineyards of the valleys. There is a deep silence over
this high frozen country. Now and then a gust of
wind brings up from the far distance the sound of
some remote waterfall or the dash of a mountain
torrent. At times, too, there comes a harsh roar as
of thunder, when some mass of ice or snow, loosened
from the rest, shoots down the precipices. But these
noises only make the silence the deeper when they
have passed away.

186. Let us see why it is that perpetual snow should
occur in such regions, and what part this snow plays
in the general machinery of the world.

187. You have learnt (Art. 96) that the higher parts
of the atmosphere are extremely cold. You know also
that in the far north and the far south, around those
two opposite parts of the earth's surface called the
Poles, the climate is extremely cold—so cold as to give
rise to dreary expanses of ice and snow, where sea and
land are frozen, and where the heat of summer is not
enough to thaw all the ice and drive away all the
snow. Between these two polar tracts of cold, wherever mountains are lofty enough to get into the high
parts of the atmosphere where the temperature is
usually below the freezing-point, the vapour condensed
from the air falls upon them, not as rain, but as snow.
Their heads and upper heights are thus covered with
perpetual snow. In such high mountainous regions
the heat of the summer always melts the snow from
the lower hills, though it leaves the higher parts still
covered. From year to year it is noticed that there is

a line or limit below which the ground gets freed of its snow, and above which the snow remains. This limit is called the **snow-line**, or the limit of **perpetual snow.** Its height varies in different parts of the world. It is highest in the warmer regions on either side of the equator, where it reaches to 15,000 feet above the sea. In the cold polar tracts, on the other hand, it approaches the sea-level. In other words, while in the polar tracts the climate is so cold that perpetual snow is found even close to the sea-level, the equatorial regions are so warm that you must climb many thousand feet before you can reach the cold layers of the air where snow can remain all the year.

188. You have no doubt watched a snow-storm. You have seen how at first a few flakes begin to show themselves drifting through the air; how they get more in number and larger in size, until the ground begins to grow white; and how, as hours go on, the whole country becomes buried under a white pall, perhaps six inches or more in thickness. You see one striking difference between rain and snow. If rain had been falling for the same length of time, the roads and fields would still have been visible, for each drop of rain, instead of remaining where it fell, would either have sunk into the soil, or have flowed off into the nearest brook. But each snowflake, on the contrary, lies where it falls, unless it happens to be caught up and driven on by the wind to some other spot where it can finally rest. Rain disappears from the ground as soon as it can; snow stays still as long as it can.

189. You will see at once that this marked differ-

ence of behaviour must give rise to some equally
strong differences in the further procedure of these
two kinds of moisture.   You have followed the progress of the rain; now let us try to find out what
becomes of the snow.

190. In such a country as ours, where there is
no perpetual snow, you can without much difficulty
answer this question.   Each fall of snow in winter-time
remains on the ground as long as the air is not warm
enough to melt it.   Evaporation, indeed, goes on from
the surface of snow and ice, as well as from water; so
that a layer of snow would in the end disappear, by
being absorbed into the air as vapour, even though none
of it had previously been melted into running water.
But it is by what we call a **thaw** that our snow is
chiefly dissipated; that is, a rise in the temperature,
and a consequent melting of the snow.   When the
snow melts, it sinks into the soil and flows off into
brooks in the same way as rain.   Its after course
needs not to be followed, for it is the same as that
of rain.   You will only bear in mind that if a
heavy fall of snow should be. quickly thawed, then
a large quantity of water will be let loose over the
country, and the brooks and rivers will rise rapidly
in flood.   Great destruction may thus be caused by
the sudden rise of rivers and the overflowing of their
banks.

191. In the regions of perpetual snow the heat of
summer cannot melt all the snow which falls there in
the year.   What other way of escape, then, can the
frozen moisture find?   That it must have some means
of taking itself off the mountains is clear enough; for
if it had not, and if it were to accumulate there from

year to year and from century to century, then the
mountains would grow into vast masses of snow, reaching far into the sky, and spreading out on all sides,
so as to bury by degrees the low lands around. But
nothing of this kind takes place. These solemn
snowy heights wear the same unchanged look from
generation to generation. There is no burying of
their well-known features under a constantly increasing depth of snow.

192. You will remember that the surplus rainfall
flows off by means of rivers. Now the surplus
snow-fall above the snow-line has a similar kind of
drainage. It flows off by means of what are called
Glaciers.

193. When a considerable depth of snow has accu-
mulated, the pressure upon the lower layers from
what lies above them squeezes them into a firm
mass. The surface of the ground is usually sloped
in some direction, seldom quite flat. And among
the high mountains the slopes are often, as you
know, very steep. When snow gathers deeply on
sloping ground, there comes a time when the force
of gravity overcomes the tendency of the pressed
snow to remain where it is, and then the snow
begins to slide slowly down the slope. From one
slope it passes on downwards to the next, joined
continually by other sliding masses from neighbouring slopes until they all unite into one long tongue
which creeps slowly down some valley to a point
where it melts. This tongue from the snow-fields is
the glacier. It really drains these snow-fields of their
excess of snow as much as a river drains a district of
its excess of water.

194 But the glacier which comes out of the snow-fields is itself made not of snow, but of ice. The snow, as it slides downward, is pressed together into ice. You have learned that each snowflake is made of little crystals of ice. A mass of snow is thus only a mass of minute crystals of ice with air between. Hence when the snow gets pressed together, the air is squeezed out, and the separated crystals of ice freeze together into a solid mass. You know that you can make a snowball very hard by squeezing it firmly between the hands. The more tightly you press it the harder it gets. You are doing to it just what happens when a glacier is formed out of the eternal snows. You are pressing out the air, and allowing the little particles of ice to freeze to each other and form a compact piece of ice. But you cannot squeeze nearly all the air out, consequently the ball, even after all your efforts, is still white from the imprisoned air. Among the snowfields, however, the pressure is immensely greater than yours ; the air is more and more pressed out, and at last the snow becomes clear transparent ice.

195. A glacier, then, is a river, not of water, but of ice, coming down from the snow-fields. It descends sometimes a long way below the snow-line, creeping down very slowly along the valley which it covers from side to side. Its surface all the time is melting during the day in summer, and streams of clear water are gushing along the ice, though, when night comes, these streams freeze. At last it reaches some point in the valley beyond which it cannot go, for the warmth of the air there is melting the ice as fast as it advances. So the glacier ends, and from its

melting extremity streams of muddy water unite into
a foaming river, which bears down the drainage of
the snow-fields above.

196. In the accompanying woodcut (fig. 13) some of
the chief characters of a glacier are shown. In the distance rise the snowy heights, among which the snow-

FIG. 13.—View of a Glacier, with its Moraines, Perched Blocks of rock, ice-
worn Bosses of rock and escaping River.

fields lie. From either side the snow is drained off
into the main valley, where it forms the glacier, which
winds with all the windings of the valley till it ends
abruptly, as you see, and a river rushes out from the
melting end of the ice.

197. A river wears down the sides and bottom of
its channel, and thus digs out a bed for itself in even

the hardest rock, as well as in the softest soil
(Art. 173). It sweeps down, too, a vast quantity of
mud, sand, and stones from the land to the sea
(Art. 172). A glacier performs the same kind of
work, but in a very different way.

198. When stones fall into a river they sink to the
bottom, and are pushed along there by the current.
When mud enters a river it remains suspended in the
water, and is thus carried along. But the ice of a
glacier is a solid substance. Stones and mud which
fall upon its surface remain there, and are borne
onward with the whole mass of the moving glacier.
They form long lines of rubbish upon the glacier, as
shown in fig. 13, and are called **moraines**. Still
the ice often gets broken up into deep cracks, opening
into yawning clefts or **crevasses**, which sometimes
receive a good deal of the earth and stones let loose
by frost or otherwise from the sides of the valley. In
this way loose materials fall to the bottom of the ice,
and reach the solid floor of the valley down which the
ice is moving; while at the same time similar rubbish
tumbles between the edge of the glacier and the side
of the valley.

199. The stones and grains of sand which get jammed
between the ice and the rock over which it is moving
are made to score and scratch this rock. They form
a kind of rough polishing powder, whereby the glacier
is continually grinding down the bottom and sides of
its channel. If you creep in below the ice, or catch a
sight of some part of the side from which the ice has
retired a little, you will find the surface of the rock all
rubbed away and covered with long scratches made
by the sharp points of the stones and sand. Some of

the rounded ice-worn bosses of rock are shown in the fore-ground of the diagram (fig. 13).

. 200. You will now see the reason why the river, which escapes from the end of a glacier, is always muddy. The bottom of the glacier is stuck all over with stones, which are scraping and wearing down the rock underneath. A great deal of fine mud is thus produced, which, carried along by streams of water flowing in channels under the glacier, emerges at the far end in the discoloured torrents which there sweep from under the ice.

FIG. 14.—Loose stone polished and scratched under glacier-ice.

201. A glacier is not only busy grinding out a bed for itself through the mountains ; it bears on its back down the valley enormous quantities of fallen rock, earth, and stones, which have tumbled from the cliffs on either side. In this way blocks of rock as big as a house may be carried for many miles, and dropped where the ice melts. In the following figure (fig. 15) you have a drawing of one of these huge masses of stone. Thousands of tons of loose stones and mud are every year moved on the ice from the far snowy moun-

tains away down into the valleys to which the glaciers reach.

202. The largest glaciers in the world are those of the polar regions. North Greenland, in truth, lies buried under one great glacier, which pushes long tongues of ice down the valleys and away out to sea. When a glacier advances into the sea, portions of it break off and float away as **icebergs** (fig. 16). So enormous are

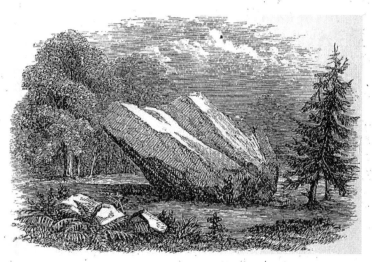

FIG. 15.—Erratic block, brought from the Alps by an ancient Glacier, and dropped upon the Jura Mountains.

the glaciers in these cold tracts that the icebergs derived from them often rise several hundred feet above the waves which beat against their sides. And yet, in all such cases, about seven times more of the ice is immersed under water than the portion, large as it is, which appears above. You can realize how this happens if you take a piece of ice, put it in a tumbler of water, and watch how much of it rises out of the water.

Sunk deep in the sea, therefore, the icebergs float to and fro until they melt, sometimes many hundreds of miles away from the glaciers which supplied them.

203. You will come to learn afterwards that, once upon a time, there were glaciers in Britain. You will be able with your own eyes to see rocks which have been ground down and scratched by the ice, and big blocks of rock and piles of loose stones which the ice

FIG. 16.—Iceberg at Sea.

carried upon its surface. In Wales, and Cumberland, in many parts of Scotland, and also in Ireland, these and many other traces of the ice are to be found. So that, in learning about glaciers, you are not merely learning what takes place in other and distant lands, you are gaining knowledge which you will be able by and by to make good use of, even in your own country.

THE SEA.

I. Grouping of Sea and Land.

204. Since we live on land, and are familiar with the various shapes which the surface of the land assumes,—plains, valleys, hills, mountains, and so on, —we are apt to think that the land is the main part of the globe. Many of us who live in the inland parts of the country have never been off the land, nor seen any larger sheet of water than a river or a lake, or perhaps a large reservoir. And yet, if you were to travel onward in any direction in Great Britain, you would at last come to the edge of the land, and find a vast expanse of water before you. If you took your place in a ship, you could sail on that water completely round this country, and you would prove in so doing that Britain is an **island**.

205. Suppose that instead of sailing round Britain, which you could easily do in a few weeks, you were to steer straight westward. You would have to travel over the water for more than two thousand miles before you reached any land again. Or, if you directed your ship in a more southerly course, you might sail on without seeing any land for months together, until you came in sight of the ice-cliffs that border the land round the South Pole. You would learn in this way what an enormous extent of the surface of the earth is occupied by water.

206. It has been ascertained that in reality the water covers about three times more of the earth's surface than the land does. We could not tell that merely by what we can see from any part of this country, or indeed of any country. It is because

men have sailed round the world, and have crossed it in many directions that the proportion of land and water has come to be known.

207. Take a school-globe, and turn it slowly round on its axis. You see at a glance how much larger the surface of water is than the surface of land. But you may notice several other interesting things about the distribution of land and water.

208. In the first place, you will find that the water is all connected together into one great mass, which we call the **sea**. The land, on the other hand, is much broken up by the way the sea runs into it; and some parts are cut off from the main mass of land, so as to form islands in the sea. Britain is one of the pieces of land so cut off.

209. In the second place, you cannot fail to notice how much more land lies on the north than on the south side of the equator. If you turn the globe so that your eye shall look straight down on the site of London, you will find that most of the land on the globe comes into sight; whereas, if you turn the globe exactly round, and look straight down on the area of New Zealand, you will see most of the sea. London thus stands about the centre of the land-hemisphere, midway among the countries of the earth. And no doubt this central position has not been without its influence in fostering the progress of British commerce.

210. In the third place, you will notice that by the way in which the masses of land are placed, parts of the sea are to some extent separated from each other. These masses of land are called **continents**, and the wide sheets of water between are termed **oceans**.

Picture to yourselves that the surface of the solid part of the earth is uneven, some portions rising into broad swellings and ridges, others sinking into wide hollows and basins. Now, into these hollows the sea has been gathered, and only those upstanding parts which rise above the level of the sea form the land.

211. In the foregoing parts of this little book mention has often been made of the Sea. You have been told that the moisture of the air comes in great part from the sea; that the rivers of the land are continually flowing into the same reservoir of water, which is likewise the great basin into which all the soil which is worn from the surface of the land is carried. We must now look a little more closely at some of the more important features of the sea.

II. Why the Sea is Salt.

212. When you come to examine the water of the sea, you find that it differs from the water with which you are familiar on the land, inasmuch as it is salt. It contains something which you do not notice in ordinary spring or river water. If you take a drop of clear spring-water, and allow it to evaporate from a piece of glass, you will find no trace left behind. The water of springs, as you have already learnt (Art. 117), always contains some mineral substances dissolved in it, and these not being capable of rising in vapour are left behind when the water evaporates. But the quantity of them in a single drop of water is so minute that, when the drop dries up, it leaves no perceptible speck or film. Take, however, a drop of sea-water, and allow it to evaporate. You find a little white point or film left behind, and on placing that

film under a microscope you see it to consist of delicate crystals of common or sea salt. It would not matter from what ocean you took the drop of water, it would still show the crystals of salt on being evaporated.

213. There are some other things besides common salt in sea-water. But the salt is the most abundant, and we need not trouble about the rest at present. Now, where did all this mineral matter in the sea come from? **The salt of the sea is all derived from the waste of the rocks.**

214. It has already been pointed out (Arts. 125, 132) how, both under ground and on the surface of the land, water is always dissolving out of the rocks various mineral substances, of which salt is one. Hence the water of springs and rivers contains salt, and this is borne away into the sea. So that all over the world there must be a vast quantity of salt carried into the ocean every year.

215. The sea gives off again by evaporation as much water as it receives from rain and from the rivers of the land. But the salt carried into it remains behind. If you take some salt water and evaporate it, the pure water disappears, and the salt is left. So it is with the sea. Streams are every day carrying fresh supplies of salt into the sea. Every day, too, millions of tons of water are passing from the ocean into vapour in the atmosphere. The waters of the sea must consequently be getting salter by degrees. The process, however, is an extremely slow one.

216. Although sea-water has probably been gradually growing in saltness ever since rivers first flowed into the great sea, it is even now by no means as salt as it might be. In the Atlantic Ocean, for example, the

total quantity of the different salts amounts only to
about three and a half parts in every hundred parts
of water. But in the Dead Sea, which is extremely
salt, the proportion is as much as twenty-four parts in
the hundred of water.

III. The Motions of the Sea.

217. Standing by the shore of any part of Britain,
and watching for a little the surface of the sea, you
notice how restless it is. Even on the calmest summer
day, a slight ripple or a gentle heaving motion will be
seen; at other times little wavelets curl towards the
land, and break in long lines upon the beach; but
now and then, when storms arise, you may watch how
the water has been worked up into huge billows which,
crested with spray, come in, tossing and foaming, to
burst upon the shores.

218. Again, if you watch a little longer, you will find
that whether the sea is calm or rough, it does not
remain always at the same limit upon the beach. At
one part of the day the edge of the water reaches to
the upper part of the sloping beach; some six hours
afterwards it has retired to the lower part. You may
watch it falling and rising, day after day, and year
after year, with so much regularity that its motion can
be predicted long beforehand. This **ebb** and **flow** of
the sea forms what are called **tides.**

219. If you cork up an empty bottle and throw it
into the sea, it will of course float. But it will not
remain long where it fell. It will begin to move
away, and may travel for a long distance until thrown
upon some shore again. Bottles cast upon mid-ocean
have been known to be carried in this way for many

hundreds of miles.   This **surface-drift** of the sea-water corresponds generally with the direction in which the prevalent winds blow.

220. But it is not merely the surface-water which moves.   You have learnt a little about icebergs (Art. 202); and one fact about them which you must remember is that, large as they may seem, there is about seven times more of their mass below water than above it.   Now, it sometimes happens that an iceberg is seen sailing on, even right in the face of a strong wind.   This shows that it is moving, not with the wind, but with a strong under-current in the sea.   In short, the sea is found to be traversed by many **currents**, some flowing from cold to warm regions, and others from warm to cold.

221. Here, then, are four facts about the sea :— 1st, it has a restless surface, disturbed by ripples and waves ; 2ndly, it is constantly heaving with the ebb and flow of the tides ; 3rdly, its surface-waters drift with the wind ; and 4thly, it possesses currents like the atmosphere.

222. For the present it will be enough if we learn something regarding the first of these facts—**the waves of the sea.**

223. Here again you may profitably illustrate by familiar objects what goes on upon so vast a scale in nature.   Take a basin, or a long trough of water, and blow upon the water at one edge.   You throw its surface into ripples, which, as you will observe, start from the place where your breath first hits the water and roll onward until they break in little wavelets upon the opposite margin of the basin.

224. What you do in a small way is the same action

by which the waves of the sea are formed.   All these
disturbances of the smoothness of the sea are due to
disturbances of the air.   Wind acts upon the water of
the sea as your breath does on that of the basin.
Striking the surface, it throws the water into ripples
or undulations, and in continuing to blow along the
surface it gives these additional force, until driven
on by a furious gale they grow into huge billows.

225. When waves roll in on the land, they break
one after another upon the shore, as your ripples
break upon the side of the basin.   And they continue
to roll in after the wind has fallen, in the same way
that the ripples in the basin will go on curling for a
little after you have ceased to blow.   The surface of
the sea, like that of water generally, is very sensitive.
If it is thrown into undulations, it does not become
motionless the moment the cause of disturbance has
passed away, but continues moving in the same way,
but in a gradually lessening degree, until it comes
to rest.

226. The restlessness of the surface of the sea
becomes in this way a reflection of the restlessness of
the air.   It is the constant moving to and fro of currents of air, either gentle or violent, which roughens
the sea with waves.   When the air for a time is calm
above, the sea sleeps peacefully below ; when the sky
darkens, and a tempest bursts forth, the sea is lashed
into waves, which roll in and break with enormous
force upon the land.

227. You have heard, perhaps you have even seen,
something of the destruction which is worked by the
waves of the sea.   Every year piers and sea-walls are
broken down, pieces of the coast are washed away,

and the shores are strewn with the wreck of ships. So that, besides all the waste which the surface of the land undergoes from rain, and frost, and streams, there is another form of destruction going on along the coast-line.

228. On rocky shores the different stages in the eating away of the land by the sea can sometimes be strikingly seen. Above the beach perhaps rises a cliff, sorely battered about its base by the ceaseless

FIG. 17.—Coast-line worn by the Sea.

grinding of the waves. Here and there a cavern has been drilled in the solid wall, or a tunnel has been driven through some projecting headland. Not far off we may note a tall buttress of rock, once a part of the main cliff, but now separated from it by the falling in and removal of the connecting archway. And then, further off from the cliff, isolated, half-tide rocks rise to show where still older detached buttresses stood ; while away out in the sea the dash of breakers marks the site of some sunken reef, in which we see the relics of a still more ancient coast-line. On such a shore the whole process whereby the sea eats into the land seems to be laid open to our eyes.

229. On some parts of the coast-line of the east of England, where the rock is easily worn away, the sea advances on the land at a rate of two or three feet every year. Towns and villages which existed a, few centuries ago have one by one disappeared, and their sites are now a long way out under the restless waters of the North Sea. On the west coast of Ireland and Scotland, however, where the rocks are usually hard and resisting, the rate of waste has been comparatively small.

230. It would be worth your while the first time you happen to be at the coast to ascertain what means the sea takes to waste the land. This you can easily do by watching what happens on a rocky beach. Get to some sandy or gravelly part of the beach, over which the waves are breaking, and keep your eye on the water when it runs back after a wave has burst. You see all the grains of gravel and sand hurrying down the slope with the water ; and if the gravel happens to be coarse, it makes a harsh grating noise as its stones rub against each other—a noise sometimes loud enough to be heard miles away. As the next wave comes curling along, you will mark that the sand and gravel, after slackening their downward pace, are caught up by the bottom of the advancing wave and dragged up the beach again, only to be hurried down once more as the water retires to allow another wave to do the same work.

231. By this continual up and down movement of the water, the sand and stones on the beach are kept grinding against each other, as in a mill. Consequently they are worn away. The stones become smaller, until they pass into mere sand, and the sand, growing finer, is swept away out to sea and laid down at the bottom.

232. But not only the loose materials on the shore suffer in this way an incessant wear and tear, the solid rocks underneath, wherever they come to the surface, are ground down in the same process. When the waves dash against a cliff they hurl the loose stones forward, and batter the rocks with them. Here and there in some softer part, as in some crevice of the cliff, these stones gather together, and when the sea runs high they are kept whirling and grinding at the base of the cliff till, in the end, a cave is actually bored by the sea in the solid rock, very much in the same way as, you remember (Art. 174), we saw that holes are bored by a river in the bed of its channel. The stones of course are ground to sand in the process, but their place is supplied by others swept up by the waves. If you enter one of these sea-caves when the water is low, you will see how smoothed and polished its sides and roof are, and how well rounded and worn are the stones lying on its floor.

IV. The Bottom of the Sea.

233. So far as we know, the bottom of the sea is very much like the surface of the land. It has heights and hollows, lines of valleys and ranges of hills. We cannot see down to the bottom where the water is

very deep, but we can let down a long·line with a
weight tied to the end of it, and find out both how
deep the water is, and what is the nature of the
bottom, whether rock or gravel, sand, mud, or shells.
This measuring of the depths of the water is called
Sounding, and the weight at the end of the line
goes by the name of the **Sounding-lead**.

234. Soundings have been made over many parts
of the sea, and something is now known about its
bottom, though much still remains to be discovered.
The Atlantic Ocean is the best known. In sounding
it, before laying down the telegraphic cable which
stretches across under the sea from this country to
America, a depth of 14,500 feet, or two miles and
three-quarters, was reached. But between the Azores
and the Bermudas a sounding has been obtained of
seven miles and a half. If you could lift up the
Himalaya mountains, which are the highest on the
globe, reaching a height of 29,000 feet above the sea,
and set them down in the deepest part of the Atlantic,
they would not only sink out of sight, but their tops
would actually be about two miles below the surface.

235. A great part of the wide sea must be one or
two miles deep. But it is not all so deep as that, for
even in mid-ocean some parts of its bottom rise up to
the surface and form islands. As a rule it deepens in
the tracts furthest from land, and shallows towards
the land. Hence those parts of the sea which run
in among islands and promontories are, for the most
part, comparatively shallow. To the west of the
island of Great Britain, stretches the wide Atlantic
Ocean ; to the east lies the much smaller North Sea ;
the former soon getting very deep as we sail west-

wards across it, the latter never deepening much even over its middle parts, which are nowhere so much as 400 feet below the surface. You may get some notion of the shallowness of the sea between this country and France, when you are told that if you could lift St. Paul's cathedral from London, and set it down in the middle of the Strait of Dover, more than a half of the building would be out of the water.

236. You may readily enough understand how it is that soundings are made, though you can see how difficult it must be to work· a sounding-line several miles long. Yet men are able not only to measure the depth of the water, but by means of the instrument called a **dredge,** to bring up bucketfuls of whatever may be lying on the sea-floor, from even the deepest parts of the ocean. In this way during the last few years a great deal of additional knowledge has been gathered as to the nature of the sea-floor, and the kind of plants and animals which live there. We now know that even in some of the deepest places which have yet been dredged there is plenty of animal life, such as shells, corals, star-fishes, and still more humble creatures.

237. In earlier parts of this book we have traced some of the changes which from day to day take place upon the surface of the land. Let us now try to watch some of those which go on upon the floor of the sea. We cannot, indeed, examine the sea-bottom with anything like the same minuteness as the surface of the land. Yet a great deal may be learnt regarding it.

238. If you put together some of the acts with which we have been dealing in the foregoing

Lessons, you may for yourselves make out some of the most important changes which are in progress on the floor of the sea. For example, try to think what must become of all the wasted rock which is every year removed from the surface of the land. It is carried into the sea by streams, as you have now learnt. But what happens to it when it gets there? From the time when it was loosened from the sides of the mountains, hills, or valleys, this decomposed material has been seeking, like water, to reach a lower level. On reaching the hollows of the sea-bottom it cannot descend any further, but must necessarily accumulate there.

239. It is evident, then, that between the floor of the sea and the surface of the land, there must be this great difference : that whereas the land is undergoing a continual destruction of its surface, from mountain-crest to sea-shore, the sea-bottom, on the other hand, is constantly receiving fresh materials on its surface. The one is increased in proportion as the other is diminished. So that even without knowing anything regarding what men have found out by means of deep soundings, you could confidently assert that every year there must be vast quantities of gravel, sand, and mud laid down upon the floor of the sea, because you know that these materials are worn away from the land.

240. Again, you have learnt that the restless agitation of the sea is due to movements of the air, and that the destruction which the sea can effect on the land is due chiefly to the action of the waves caused by wind. But this action must be merely a surface one. The influence of the waves cannot reach to

the bottom of the deep sea. Consequently that bottom lies beyond the reach of the various kinds of destruction which so alter the face of the land. The materials which are derived from the waste of the land can lie on the sea-floor without further disturbance than they may suffer from the quiet flow of such ocean currents as touch the bottom.

241. In what way, then, are the gravel, sand, and mud disposed of when they reach the sea?

242. As these materials are all brought from the land, they accumulate on those parts of the sea-floor which border the land, rather than at a distance. We may expect to find banks of sand and gravel in shallow seas and near land, but not in the middle of the ocean.

243. You may form some notion, on a small scale, as to how the materials are arranged on the sea-bottom, by examining the channel of a river in a season of drought. At one place, where the current has been strong, there may be a bank of gravel; at another place, where the currents of the river have met, you will find, perhaps, a ridge of sand which they have heaped up; while in those places where the flow of the stream has been more gentle, the channel may be covered with a layer of fine silt or mud. You remember that a muddy river may be made to deposit its mud if it overflows its banks so far as to spread over flat land which checks its flow (Art. 178).

244. The more powerful a current of water, the larger will be the stones it can move along. Hence coarse gravel is not likely to be found over the bottom of the sea, except near the land, where the waves can

sweep it out into the path of strong sea-currents. Sand will be carried further out, and laid down in great sheets, or in banks. The finer mud and silt may be borne ' by currents for hundreds of miles before at last settling down upon the sea-bottom.

245. In this way, according to the nearness of the land and the strength of the ocean-currents, the sand, mud, and gravel worn from the land are spread out in vast sheets and banks over the bottom of the sea.

246. But the sea is full of life, both of plants and animals. These organisms die, and their remains necessarily get mixed up with the different materials laid down upon the sea-floor. So that, besides the mere sand and mud, great numbers of shells, corals, and the harder parts of other sea-creatures must be buried there, as generation after generation comes and goes.

247. It often happens that on parts of the sea-bed the remains of some of these animals are so abundant that they themselves form thick and wide-spread deposits. Oysters, for example, grow thickly together; and their shells, mingled with those of other similar creatures, form what are called **shell-banks**. In the Pacific and the Indian Oceans a little animal, called the coral-polyp, secretes a hard limy skeleton from the sea-water; and as millions of these polyps grow together, they form great reefs of solid rock, which are sometimes, as in the Great Barrier Reef of Australia, hundreds of feet thick and a thousand miles long. It is by means of the growth of these animals that those wonderful rings of coral-rock or **Coral-islands** (Fig. 18) are formed in the middle of the ocean. Again, a great part of

the bed of the Atlantic Ocean is covered with fine mud, which on examination is found to consist almost wholly of the remains of very minute animals called Foraminifera.

FIG. 18.—Island formed by the Growth of Coral.

248. Over the bottom of the sea, therefore, great beds of sand and mud, mingled with the remains of plants and animals, are always accumulating. If now this bottom could be raised up above the sea-level, even though the sand and mud should get as dry and hard as any rock among the hills, you would be able to say with certainty that they had once been under the sea, because you would find in them the shells and other remains of marine animals.

249. You will afterwards learn when you come to the science of Geology that this raising of the sea-bottom has often taken place in ancient times. You will find most of the rocks of our hills and valleys to have been originally laid down in the sea, where they were formed out of sand and mud dropped on the sea-floor, just as sand and mud are carried out to sea and laid down there now. And in these rocks, not merely near the shore, but far inland, in quarries or ravines,

or the sides and even the tops of hills, you will be able to pick out the skeletons and fragments of the various sea-creatures which were living in the old seas.'

250. Since the bottom of the sea forms the great receptacle into which the mouldered remains of the surface of the land are continually carried, it is plain that if this state of things were to go on without modification or hindrance, in the end the whole of the solid land would be worn away, and its remains would be spread out on the sea-floor, leaving one vast ocean to roll round the globe.

251. But there is in nature another force which here comes into play to retard the destruction of the land. We must in the remaining Lessons of this book consider what this force is, and how it works.

THE INSIDE OF THE EARTH.

252. In the foregoing pages your attention has been given to the surface of the earth, and what goes on there. Let us now consider for a little what can be learnt regarding the inside of the earth.

253. It may seem, at first, as if it were hopeless that man should ever know anything about the earth's interior. Just think what a huge ball this globe of ours is, and you will see that after all, in living and moving over its surface, we are merely like flies walking over a great hill. All that can be seen from the top of the highest mountain to the bottom of the

deepest mine is not more in comparison than the mere varnish on the outside of a school-globe. And yet a good deal can be learnt as to what takes place within the earth. Here and there, in different coun-tries, there are places where communication exists between the interior and the surface; and it is from such places that much of our information on this subject is derived.

254. You have, no doubt, read of **Volcanoes** or **Burning-mountains** (fig. 19). These are among the most important of the channels of communication with the interior.

255. Let us suppose that you were to visit one of these volcanoes just before what is called "an eruption." As you approach it, you see a conical mountain, seem-ingly with its top cut off. From this truncated sum-mit a white cloud rises. But it is not quite such a cloud as you would see on a hill-top in this country. For as you watch it you notice that it rises out of the top of the mountain, even though there are no clouds to be seen anywhere else. Ascending from the vegetation of the lower grounds, you find the slopes to consist partly of loose stones and ashes, partly of rough black sheets of rock, like the slags of an iron furnace. As you get nearer the top the ground feels hot, and puffs of steam, together with stifling vapours, come out of it here and there. At last you reach the summit, and there what seemed a level top is seen to be in reality a great basin, with steep walls descending into the depths of the mountain. Screening your face as well as possible from the hot gases which almost choke you, you creep to the top of this basin, and look down into it. Far below, at

10

the base of the rough red and yellow cliffs which form its sides, lies a pool of some liquid, glowing with a white heat, though covered for the most part with a black crust like that seen on the outside of the mountain during the ascent. From this fiery pool jets of the red-hot liquid are jerked out every now and

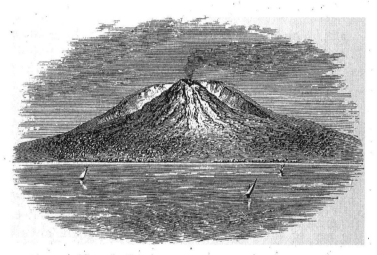

Fig. 19.—View of a Volcano. Mount Vesuvius as it appears at the present time, when viewed from the south.

then, stones and dust are cast up into the air, and fall back again, and clouds of steam ascend from the same source and form the uprising cloud which is seen from a great distance hanging over the mountain.

256. This caldron-shaped hollow on the summit of the mountain is the **Crater**. The intensely heated liquid in the sputtering boiling pool at its bottom is melted rock or **Lava**. And the fragmentary materials —ashes, dust, cinders, and stones—thrown out, are torn from the hardened sides and bottom of the crater

by the violence of the explosions with which the gases and steam escape.

257. The hot air and steam, and the melted mass at the bottom of the crater, show that there must be some source of intense heat underneath. And as the heat has been coming out for hundreds, or even thousands of years, it must exist there in great abundance.

258. But it is when the volcano appears in active eruption that the power of this underground heat shows itself most markedly. For a day or two beforehand, the ground around the mountain trembles. At length, in a series of violent explosions, the heart of the volcano is torn open, and perhaps its upper part is blown into the air. Huge clouds of steam roll away up into the air, mingled with fine dust and red-hot stones. The heavier stones fall back again into the crater or on the outer slopes of the mountain, but the finer ashes come out in such quantity, as sometimes to darken the sky for many miles round, and to settle down over the surrounding country as a thick covering. Streams of white-hot molten lava run down the outside of the mountain, and descend even to the gardens and houses at the base, burning up or overflowing whatever lies in their path. This state of matters continues for days or weeks, until the volcano exhausts itself, and then a time of comparative quiet comes when only steam, hot vapours, and gases are given off.

259. About 1800 years ago, there was a mountain near Naples shaped like a volcano, and with a large crater covered with brushwood (fig. 20). No one had ever seen any steam, or ashes, or lava come from it, and the people did not imagine it to be a volcano, like

some other mountains in that part of Europe. They had built villages and towns around its base, and their district, from its beauty and soft climate, used to attract wealthy Romans to build villas there. But at last, after hardly any warning, the whole of the higher part of the mountain was blown into the air with terrific explosions. Such showers of fine ashes fell for miles around, that the sky was as dark as midnight. Day and night the ashes and

FIG. 20. — Vesuvius as it appeared before Pompeii was destroyed.

stones descended on the surrounding country; many of the inhabitants were killed, either by stones falling on them, or from suffocation by the dust. When at last the eruption ceased, the district, which had before drawn visitors from all parts of the old world, was found to be a mere desert of grey dust and stones. Towns and villages, vineyards and gardens, were all buried. Of the towns, the two most noted were called Herculaneum and Pompeii. So completely did they disappear, that, although important places at the time, their very sites were forgotten, and only by accident, after the lapse of some fifteen hundred years, were they discovered. Excavations have since that time been carried on, the hardened volcanic accumulations have been removed from the old city, and you can now walk through the streets of Pompeii again, with their roofless dwelling-houses and shops, theatres and temples, and mark on the causeway the deep ruts worn by the carriage wheels of the Pompeians eighteen centuries ago. Beyond the walls of the now silent city rises Mount Vesuvius, with its smoking crater, covering one-half of the old mountain which was blown up when Pompeii disappeared (See fig. 19.)

260. Volcanoes, then, mark the position of some of the holes or orifices, whereby heated materials from the inside of the earth are thrown up to the surface. They occur in all quarters of the globe. In Europe, besides Mount Vesuvius, which has been more or less active since it was formed, Etna, Stromboli, and other smaller volcanoes, occur in the basin of the Mediterranean, while far to the north-west some active volcanoes rise amid the snows and glaciers of Iceland. In America a chain of huge volcanoes stretches down the range of mountains which rises from the western margin of the continent. In Asia they are thickly grouped together in Java and some of the surrounding islands ; and stretch thence through Japan and the Aleutian Isles, to the extremity of North America. If you trace this distribution upon the map, you will see that the Pacific Ocean is girded all round with volcanoes.

261. Since these openings into the interior of the earth are so numerous over the surface, we may conclude that this interior is intensely hot.   But we have other proofs of this internal heat.   In many countries **hot springs** rise to the surface.   Even in England, which is a long way from any active volcano, the water of the wells of Bath is quite warm (120° Fahr.).   It is known, too, that in all countries the heat increases as we descend into the earth. The deeper a mine the warmer are the rocks and air at its bottom.   If the heat continues to increase in the same proportion, the rocks must be red hot at no great distance beneath us.

262. It is not merely by volcanoes and hot-springs, however, that the internal heat of the earth affects the surface.   The solid ground is made to tremble, or is rent asunder, or upheaved or let down.   You have probably heard or read of **earthquakes**: those shakings of the ground, which, when they are at their worst, crack the ground open, throw down trees and buildings, and bury hundreds or thousands of people in the ruins.   Earthquakes are most common in or near those countries where active volcanoes exist. They frequently take place just before a volcanic eruption.

263. Some parts of the land are slowly rising out of the sea ; rocks, which used always to be covered. by the tides, come to be wholly beyond their limits ; while others, which used never to be seen at all, begin one by one to show their heads above water. On the other hand some tracts are slowly sinking ; piers, sea-walls, and other old landmarks on the beach, are one after another enveloped by the sea

as it encroaches further and higher on the land. These movements, whether in an upward or downward direction, are likewise due in some way to the internal heat.

264. Now when you reflect upon these various changes you will see that through the agency of this same internal heat land is preserved upon the face of the earth. If rain and frost, rivers, glaciers, and the sea were to go on wearing down the surface of the land continually without any counterbalancing kind of action, the land would necessarily in the end disappear, and indeed would have disappeared long ago. But owing to the pushing out of some parts of the earth's surface by the movements of the heated materials inside, portions of the land are raised to a higher level, while parts of the bed of the sea are actually upheaved so as to form land.

265. This kind of elevation has happened many times in all quarters of the globe. As already mentioned (Art. 249), most of our hills and valleys are formed of rocks, which were originally laid down on the bottom of the sea, and have been subsequently raised into land.

CONCLUSION.

266. In conclusion, let us sum up the leading features of the foregoing Lessons.

267. This earth of ours is the scene of continual movement and change. The atmosphere which encircles it is continually in motion, diffusing heat, light, and vapour. From the sea and from the waters

of the land, vapour is constantly passing into the air,
whence, condensed into clouds, rain and snow, it
descends again to the earth.   All over the surface of
, the land the water which falls from the sky courses
seawards in brooks and rivers, bearing into the great
deep the materials which are worn away from the land.
Water is thus ceaselessly circulating between the air,
the land, and the sea.   The sea, too, is never at
rest.   Its waves gnaw the edges of the land, and its
currents sweep round the globe.   Into its depths the
spoils of the land are borne, there to gather into rocks,
out of which new islands and continents will even-
tually be formed.   Lastly, inside the earth is lodged a
vast store of heat by which the surface is shaken,
rent open, upraised or depressed.   Thus while old
land is submerged beneath the sea, new tracts are upheaved, to be clothed with vegetation and peopled
with animals, and to form a fitting abode for man
himself.

268. This world is not a living being, like a plant
or an animal, and yet you must now see that there
is a sense in which we may speak of it as such.   The
circulation of air and water, the interchange of sea
and land ; in short, the system of endless and continual movement by which the face of the globe is '
day by day altered and renewed, may well be called
the Life of the Earth.

QUESTIONS.

THE SHAPE OF THE EARTH, p. 8.

1. What is the first impression we have of the shape of the Earth?

2. How could you show in the interior of a level country that the apparent plain is really part of the surface of a globe?

3. Prove the same conclusion from what may be seen on the sea-coast.

4. How has the shape of the earth been tested by "circum-navigators?"

5. Show how the gentle curvature indicates the size of the globe.

6. How long would a railway train moving at a rate of thirty miles an hour take to go round the earth?

DAY AND NIGHT, p. 13.

1. Whence does the earth derive its surface-heat and light?

2. What was the ancient belief as to the relative positions of the earth, sun, moon, and stars?

3. Are there any traces of this early belief still to be found in our everyday speech?

4. What is the real relation of the sun to the earth?

5. The succession of day and night appears as if it were due to the movement of the sun across the sky; illustrate how it is really caused by the motion of the earth.

6. What is meant by the terms *axis of rotation*, *north pole* and *south pole?*

7. In what direction is the earth rotating? How is this indicated by day and at night respectively?

8. What is the earth's motion of *revolution?*

9. In what time does the earth perform a complete revolution?

10. Show how the movements of the earth determine our divisions of time.

THE AIR.

I. What the Air is made of, p. 16.

1. What is meant by the term *Atmosphere?*
2. Of what materials is the air mainly composed?
3. Besides the two chief gases, name some other substances always present in the air.
4. How may the presence of visible particles be shown?
5. What is water-vapour? [See art. 73.] Show by any familiar example how it may be invisibly dissolved in the air. [See art. 71.]
6. In what proportion does carbonic acid gas occur in the air?
7. Show how important this material is in relation to the growth of plants and animals.

II. The Warming and Cooling of the Air, p. 19.

1. In what ways are we made sensible of the presence of the air?
2. Why do we feel cold when we pass from a warm room into the outer air in winter?
3. The sun is always radiating heat to the earth; why then should there be alternations of heat and cold in the air?
4. Does the atmosphere allow the whole of the sun's heat-rays to pass through it to the surface of the earth?
5. Why is the sun's heat less felt in the morning and in the evening than at noon?
6. Why is night so much colder than day?
7. Why is summer warmer than winter?
8. Why is it that cloudy days are not always or necessarily cold?
9. Since the air absorbs only part of the heat of the sun which passes through it to the earth's surface, how is it chiefly warmed and how cooled? [See art. 64.]
10. What prevents excessive loss of heat at night by radiation?
11. Why are the nights often felt to be so cold in warm countries?
12. Why are cloudy nights usually warmer than clear ones?

III. What happens when Air is warmed or cooled. Wind, p. 24.

1. Whether is warm or cold air the heavier, and why?

2. What is the general effect of difference of density in causing movement of the air?

3. How do a red-hot poker and a common fire-place illustrate this movement?

4. How does wind arise from the unequal heating of the earth's surface?

5. Explain the nature and origin of land and sea breezes.

6. Which is the hottest belt of the earth's surface, and why?

7. Explain the nature and origin of the trade winds.

8. How does water-vapour cause movements in the atmosphere?

IV. The Vapour in the Air.   Evaporation and Condensation, p. 27.

1. Explain why a film of mist appears on a cold glass when brought into a warm room.

2. How does the capacity of the air to retain water-vapour vary according to temperature?

3. Why does a film of mist appear upon a mirror or other cold surface when it is breathed on, and what is the explanation of the cloud which issues from one's mouth with every breath in cold weather.

4. What is the dew-point?

5. How is the vapour of water brought into the air?

6. At what times is evaporation most and least vigorous?

7. Explain the cause of the chill that is felt when a drop of water is evaporated on the back of the hand?

V. Dew, Mist, Clouds, p. 31.

1. Give some examples of the condensation of vapour.

2. Explain the formation of dew.

3. Show how mists are formed upon mountains

4. Explain the origin of the fog often seen rising after sunset from the surface of a river.

5. Explain the formation of clouds.

VI. Where Rain and Snow come from, p. 35.

1. In what ways do clouds disappear from the sky?

2. Explain the formation and fall of rain.

3. Under what different forms does water present itself?

4. What is ice and when is it formed?

5. What is snow? Describe a snow-flake.

6. What are hail and sleet?

7. Describe the circulation of water between the air and the earth.

THE CIRCULATION OF WATER ON THE LAND.

I. What becomes of the Rain, p. 39

1. Why do not seas, lakes, and rivers, become visibly less, seeing that they lose so much water by evaporation?

2. What part does the sea play in supplying the air with moisture?

3. What becomes of that part of the rain which falls into the sea?

4. How much rain is estimated to fall annually upon the British Isles?

5. How is the rain which falls upon land disposed of? [See art. 106.]

6. How may it be shown that a considerable quantity of rain sinks into the ground, and yet that this quantity is not permanently removed from the circulation?

II. How Springs are formed, p. 42.

1. How do sand and clay differ from each other in regard to the passage of water through them?

2. How does this difference affect the kinds of soil?

3. What inference as to the movements of the underground water, may be drawn from the fact that water gathers in any deep hole or quarry which may be dug out of the ground?

4. What natural channels are provided for the passage of water, even through very hard rocks?

5. Explain the occurrence of boggy places in hilly ground.

6. What are springs?

7. Explain why springs issue from between beds of rock along the sides of valleys.

8. Explain the origin of deep-seated springs.

9. How is the underground circulation of water shown by wells, mines, and pits?

III. The work of Water Underground, p. 47.

1. Does clear spring-water contain anything else than water? How may this be answered practically?

2. What common solutions show that clear transparent water may contain a good deal of foreign matter invisible to the eye?

3. Whence must the substances dissolved in spring-water be derived ?

4. What part does rain play in regard to the purification of the air ?

5. Whence does rain-water derive the carbonic acid which it carries below the soil ?

6. What effect has water containing carbonic acid on many rocks ?

7. Explain this action of water in limestone countries.

8. What is the difference between hard and soft water?

9. Are the substances carried up from below in spring-water of any service in the growth of plants and animals ?

10. What is the origin of underground tunnels and caverns ?

IV. How the Surface of the Earth crumbles away, p. 51.

1. What change usually takes place upon masonry after it has been exposed for a time to the air ?

2. Show how a similar change can be observed elsewhere than in human erections.

3. Explain the part taken by carbonic acid in the crumbling of the rocks at the surface of the earth.

4. Explain the effect of the oxygen in rain-water upon iron and on many rocks.

5. Explain the action of frost in promoting the crumbling of soil and the splitting up of rocks.

6. What is the effect of rapid extremes of heat and cold upon rocks?

7. State the general result of all these destructive agents upon the surface of the land, and show how their action is beneficial in making the earth a fit dwelling-place for plants and animals.

V. What becomes of the Crumbled Parts of Rocks. How Soil is made, p. 58.

1. What is common garden soil made of?

2. What is meant by the chemical action of rain?

3. Explain the mechanical action of rain.

4. What is the nature of the process by which soil is made?

5. Explain how soil is continually renewed.

6. Show how plants lend their help in the making of soil.

7. What part do common earth-worms play in the process ?

8. In what sense may it be said that the general surface of the land is continually moving towards the sea ?

9. How do brooks and rivers illustrate the extent to which the surface of the land is mouldering?

11

VI. Brooks and Rivers.   Their Origin, p. 62.

1. Describe the formation of miniature brooks and rivers on a sloping roadway during a heavy shower of rain.
2. Why do streams flow?
3. What are lakes?
4. Why does the rain run off the surface of the land in runnels, brooks, and rivers?
5. How are the innumerable brooks of the high ground disposed of as they descend towards the lower country?
6. What is meant by a water-shed?
7. Why do rivers continue to flow even in dry weather?
8. Why are some rivers, such as the Rhine, most swollen in summer?
9. What becomes of all the surplus drainage of the land?

VII. Brooks and Rivers.   Their Work, p. 68.

1. Give an illustration of the vast amount of invisible material carried, in chemical solution, by a river to the sea.
2. Why are rivers discoloured during floods?
3. What is the origin of the gravel and blocks of stone in the bed of a stream, and why are the stones usually rounded?
4. What are pot-holes?
5. How have river gorges and ravines been formed?
6. Describe the bed of a river when the water is low.
7. Explain the origin of the flat terraces bordering a river.
8. Describe a delta, and show how it may be formed at the mouth of a river, in a lake, or in the sea.
9. What becomes of the mud and sand which are carried past the delta?

VIII. Snowfields and Glaciers, p. 75.

1. What is meant by the snow-line?
2. What is its height at the equator and in the polar regions?
3. Why does snow remain perpetual above the snow-line?
4. In what way does the snow below the snow-line disappear?
5. How may the sudden melting of snow prove very destructive?
6. What becomes of the mass of snow which accumulates above the snow-line?
7. Describe the formation of a glacier.
8. What becomes of a glacier as it descends its valley?
9. What are moraines?
10. How do stones and earth get under the ice of a glacier?
11. What use does the glacier make of these stones and particles of earth and sand?

12. Why is the river of water muddy which escapes from the end of a glacier?

13. Where do the largest glaciers exist?

14. Explain the formation of icebergs.

15. What proofs have been found that glaciers once existed in countries such as Britain, where they no longer occur?

THE SEA.

I. Grouping of Sea and Land, p. 86.

1. What are the proportions of land and water on the earth's surface?

2. Mention the broad difference between sea and land in the way they are distributed over the globe.

3. On which side of the equator does most of the land lie?

4. What part of the earth's surface lies in the centre of the land hemisphere?

5. What are continents and islands?

6. What are oceans?

II. Why the Sea is Salt, p. 88.

1. In what familiar respect does the water of the sea differ from that of ordinary springs and rivers?

2. What happens when a drop of sea-water is evaporated on a piece of glass?

3. Whence has the mineral matter in sea-water come?

4. What is the relative saltness of the Atlantic Ocean and the Dead Sea?

III. The Motions of the Sea, p. 90.

1. What is the commonest and most obvious form of motion in the sea?

2. How does the ebb and flow of the tides show itself on a sloping beach?

3. What is surface drift, and how is it often indicated?

4. What are currents in the sea, and how are they sometimes made evident?

5. How may a basin or trough of water be made to illustrate the formation of waves?

6. What is the connection between movements of the air and ripples or waves on the sea?

7. What general effect have waves on the edge of the land exposed to their influence?

8. Explain the process by which gravel and sand are ground down by the waves upon the beach.

9. How do the waves wear down a rocky coast?

IV. The Bottom of the Sea, p. 95.

1. What is the general character of the sea-floor as compared with the surface of the land?

2. How is our information regarding the bottom of the deep sea obtained?

3. What was found to be the depth of the Atlantic Ocean when soundings were made for the telegraphic cable between Britain and America?

4. What is the greatest depth that has yet been observed in the Atlantic, and where does it occur?

5. What is the depth of a great part of the sea?

6. Which are usually the deepest and which the shallowest parts of the sea?

7 What is the depth of the deeper parts of the North Sea?

8. How much of St. Paul's Cathedral in London would be submerged were it placed in the middle of the Straits of Dover?

9. What is a *dredge*, and what use is made of it?

10. What light has been obtained by means of the dredge regarding the living things of the deep sea bottom?

11 Mention an important difference between the crumbling land-surface described in a former lesson [arts. 123—142], and the bottom of the sea.

12. To what part of the sea is the destructive action of the waves limited?

13. How are the mud, earth, sand, and gravel disposed of which the sea obtains from the crumbling surface of the land?

14. What becomes of the remains of the shells, corals, and other creatures on the sea-floor?

15. What are shell-banks?

16. What are coral-reefs and coral-islands, and how are they formed?

17. What is the nature of the mud which covers a great part of the bed of the Atlantic?

18. How could you be certain that some rocks must once have been under the sea?

THE INSIDE OF THE EARTH, p. 102

1. Does the distance from the top of the highest mountain to the bottom of the deepest mine bear a large proportion to the diameter of the whole globe?

2. What is a volcano?

3. What various materials are thrown out by a volcano?

4. What evidence do these materials furnish as to the condition of the earth's interior?

5. Describe a volcanic eruption.

6. What has been the history of Vesuvius?

7. State the position of some of the volcanoes of Europe, America, and Asia.

8. What evidence do hot springs bring to bear upon the state of the internal parts of our globe?

9. What has been observed regarding temperature as we descend into the earth, and what inference has been drawn from it?

10. What are earthquakes? Where are they most frequent?

11. Mention any facts which show that different parts of the earth's surface are slowly changing their level.

12. In what way does the action of the earth's internal heat tend to counteract the general lowering of level caused by the destructive action of air, rain, frosts, rivers, glaciers, and the sea?

13. Under what circumstances were the rocks of most of our hills and valleys formed?

THE END.

PRIMERS

IN SCIENCE, HISTORY, AND LITERATURE.

18mo. . . Flexible cloth, 45 cents each.

SCIENCE PRIMERS.

Edited by Professors HUXLEY, ROSCOE, and BALFOUR
STEWART.

Introductory..T. H. HUXLEY.
Chemistry......H. E. ROSCOE.
Physics...BALFOUR STEWART.
Physical Geography....A.
GEIKIE.
Geology...........A. GEIKIE.
Physiology.......M. FOSTER.
Astronomy...J. N. LOCKYER.
Botany.........J. D. HOOKER.
Logic...... .....W. S. JEVONS.

Inventional Geometry.W.
G. SPENCER.
Pianoforte...FRANKLIN TAY-
LOR.
Political Economy...W. S.
JEVONS.
Natural Resources of the
United States. J. H. PAT-
TON.

HISTORY PRIMERS.

Edited by J. R. GREEN, M. A., Examiner in the School of Mod-
ern History at Oxford.

Greece ....C. A. FYFFE.
Rome..........M. CREIGHTON.
Europe........E. A. FREEMAN.
Old Greek Life.J.P. MAHAFFY.

Roman Antiquities...A. S.
WILKINS.
Geography...GEORGE GROVE.

LITERATURE PRIMERS.

Edited by J. R. GREEN, M. A.

English Grammar.......R.
MORRIS.
English Literature...STOP-
FORD A. BROOKE.
Philology...........J. PEILE.
Classical Geography....M.
F. TOZER.
Shakespeare....E. DOWDEN.

Studies in Bryant.J. ALDEN.
Greek Literature.R. C. JEBB.
English Grammar Exer-
cises..............R. MORRIS.
Homer.....W. E. GLADSTONE.
English Composition....J.
NICHOL.

(Others in preparation.)

The object of these primers is to convey information in such a
manner as to make it both intelligible and interesting to very young
pupils, and so to discipline their minds as to incline them to more
systematic after-studies. The woodcuts which illustrate them em-
bellish and explain the text at the same time.

D. APPLETON & CO., Publishers,
1, 3, & 5 BOND STREET, NEW YORK.

INTERNATIONAL · SCIENTIFIC SERIES.

D. APPLETON & CO., Publishers, 1, 3, & 5 Bond St., N. Y.

NEW BOOKS.

I.

APPLETONS' SUMMER BOOK. A Unique Volume for the Traveler by Rail or Steamboat, or the Country Sojourner at the Seaside, in the Mountains, or wherever he may be. Contains Stories and Sketches suitable for the Season, and a Great Number of Articles on Summer Topics.

"'Appletons' Summer Book' contains a large amount of very interesting and instructive reading in the form of timely papers dealing with summer topics. There are also articles on 'Our Summer Pleasure-Places,' by O. B. Bunce; 'About Fishing,' by Barnet Phillips; 'A Trip up the Hudson,' by C. H. Jones; 'Vacation in Colorado,' by W. H. Rideing; 'Summer Pictures,' by O. B. Bunce; and other papers by George Cooper, Ernest Ingersoll, R. R. Bowker, Nugent Robinson, C. E. Craddock, and others; and poems by E. C. Stedman, George Edgar Montgommery. and A. B. Street. The book is copiously and admirably illustrated, and the whole proves a capital collection of light and pleasing amusement for an idle afternoon."—*Boston Gaz.*

Superbly illustrated, with an exquisite Design engraved on Steel for the Cover. Large 8vo. Price, 50 cents.

II.

A THOUSAND FLASHES OF FRENCH WIT, WISDOM, AND WICKEDNESS. Collected and translated by J. DE FINOD. One vol., 16mo. Cloth. Price, $1.00.

This work consists of a collection of wise and brilliant sayings from French writers, making a rich and piquant book of fresh quotations.
"The book is a charming one to take up for an idle moment during the warm weather, and is just the thing to read on the hotel piazza to a mixed company of ladies and gentlemen. Some of its sayings about the first mentioned would no doubt occasion lively discussion, but that is just what is needed to dispel the often wellnigh intolerable languor of a summer afternoon."—*Boston Courier.*

III.

MEMORIES OF MY EXILE. By LOUIS KOSSUTH. Translated from the original Hungarian by FERENCZ JAUSZ. One vol., crown 8vo. Cloth. Price, $2 00.

"A most piquant and instructive contribution to contemporary history."—*New York Sun.*
"These 'Memories' disclose a curious episode in the inner life of English domestic politics."—*The Nation.*

D. APPLETON & CO., PUBLISHERS, 1, 5, & 5 BOND STREET, N. Y.

IV.

EDUCATION: INTELLECTUAL, MORAL, AND PHYSICAL. By HERBERT SPENCER. A new cheap edition of Herbert Spencer's famous Essays on Education. 1 vol., 12mo, paper cover. Price, 50 cents.

V.

THE BRAIN AS AN ORGAN OF MIND. By H. CHARLTON BASTIAN, Professor of Anatomy and Clinical Medicine in University College, London; author of " Paralysis from Brain Disease." With numerous Illustrations. 1 vol., 12mo, 708 pages. Cloth. Price, $2.50.

"The fullest scientific exposition yet published of the views held on the subject of psychology by the advanced physiological school. It teems with new and suggestive ideas; and, though the author displays throughout his customary boldness of speculation, he does not allow himself to be carried away so freely as of old by his own exuberant wealth of 'scientific imagination.'"—*London Athenæum.*

VI.

SECOND VOLUME OF

COOLEY'S CYCLOPÆDIA OF PRACTICAL RECEIPTS. Cooley's Cyclopædia of Practical Receipts and Collateral Information in the Arts, Manufactures, Professions, and Trades, etc., etc. Sixth edition, revised and partly rewritten by Professor RICHARD V. TUSON. Volume two, completing the work, now ready. 8vo, 1,796 pages (complete). Price, $4.50 per volume.

VII.

A HISTORY OF PHILOSOPHY IN EPITOME. By ALBERT SCHWEGLER. Translated from the first edition of the original German by Julius H. Seelye. Revised from the ninth German edition, containing Important Additions and Modifications, with an Appendix, continuing the History in its more Prominent Lines of Development since the Time of Hegel, by Benjamin T. Smith. 12mo, 469 pages. Cloth. Price, $2.00.

VIII.

LIVY. By the Rev. W. W. CAPES, M. A. Fifth volume in "CLASSICAL WRITERS." 16mo, flexible. Price, 60 cents. Previously published in the series: "Milton," "Euripides," "Sophocles," "Vergil." Uniform style. 60 cents each.

D. APPLETON & CO., PUBLISHERS, 1, 3, & 5 BOND STREET, N. Y.

IX.

LITTLE COMEDIES. By JULIAN STURGIS, author of "John-a-Dreams," "An Accomplished Gentleman," etc. "New Handy-Volume Series." Paper, 30 cents.

"They are light, sparkling, piquant. and amusing. They hit off, in the course of conversations carried on between men and women of the world, social foibles with a wit remarkable for its keenness. . . . On a hot summer's day they would make peculiarly delicious reading —not too exhilarating, but softly, pleasantly flowing along."—*London Standard.*

X.

FRENCH MEN OF LETTERS. Personal and Anecdotical Sketches of VICTOR HUGO; ALFRED DE MUSSET; THÉOPHILE GAUTIER; HENRI MURGER; SAINTE-BEUVE; GÉRARD DE NERVAL; ALEXANDRE DUMAS, FILS; ÉMILE AUGIER; OCTAVE FEUILLET; VICTORIEN SARDOU; ALPHONSE DAUDET; and ÉMILE ZOLA. By MAURICE MAURIS. Appletons' "New Handy-Volume Series." Paper, 35 cents.

"A notable addition is made to Appletons' admirable 'New Handy-Volume Series,' in 'French Men of Letters,' by Maurice Mauris. It is a delightful book, containing a dozen sketches of the great men whose names are known to all the world, but whose personalities, for the most part, the world only guesses at. The little book really is charming: as good reading as a good novel, and above even the best of novels in that its characters are real."—*Philadelphia Times.*

XI.

A SHORT LIFE OF WILLIAM EWART GLADSTONE. With Extracts from his Speeches and Writings. By CHARLES H. JONES, author of "Lord Macaulay: his Life, his Writings," "A Short Life of Charles Dickens," etc. Appletons' "New Handy-Volume Series." Paper, 35 cents.

XII.

THE FORESTERS. By BERTHOLD AUERBACH. Appletons' "New Handy-Volume Series." Paper, 50 cents.

For sale by all booksellers ; or any work sent by mail, post-paid, on receipt of price.

D. APPLETON & CO., Publishers,

1, 3, & 5 BOND STREET, NEW YORK.

QUACKENBOS'S
NATURAL PHILOSOPHY.

A NATURAL PHILOSOPHY: embracing the most recent Discoveries in the Various Branches of Physics, and exhibiting the Application of Scientific Principles in Every-day Life. Adapted to use with or without Apparatus, and accompanied with Practical Exercises and Numerous Illustrations. By G. P. QUACKENBOS, LL. D. *Revised edition* (1871). 12mo. 450 pages. $1.50.

CORNELL'S PHYSICAL GEOGRAPHY.

A PHYSICAL GEOGRAPHY: accompanied with Nineteen Pages of Maps, a great Variety of Map-Questions, and One Hundred and Thirty Diagrams and Pictorial Illustrations; and embracing a detailed Description of the Physical Features of the United States. By S. S. CORNELL. Large 4to. 104 pages. $1.40.

HUXLEY & YOUMANS'S PHYSIOLOGY.

THE ELEMENTS OF PHYSIOLOGY AND HYGIENE. A Text-Book for Educational Institutions. By THOMAS H. HUXLEY, F. R. S., and WILLIAM JAY YOUMANS, M. D. 12mo. 420 pages. $1.50.

Prof. Huxley ranks among the first of living physiologists, and his opinions are received with deference by the most advanced minds. This book was written by him for the purpose of clearing the subject from the crude statements and doubtful doctrines which had crept into the popular text-books through the incompetence of compilers.

The general subject of Hygiene, prepared by Dr. Youmans, is treated in a series of chapters, bearing the following titles: The Scope and Aim of Hygiene; Air and Health; Water and Health; Food and Health; Clothing and Health; Exercise and Health; Mental Hygiene.

D. APPLETON & CO., PUBLISHERS,
NEW YORK.

CPSIA information can be obtained
at www.ICGtesting.com
Printed in the USA
LVHW080304030919
629674LV00014B/1204/P